# THE INSIDE OUT STORY

*DISCOVERING STRUCTURE FOR SHORT FILMS*

*BY*

*JOHN BUCHER & JEREMY CASPER*

8033 Sunset Blvd. #164
Los Angeles, CA. 90046
sideshowmediagroup.com

Published in Los Angeles, California, by Sideshow Media Group

Bulk copies of this book can be ordered by contacting:

Sideshow Media Group
8033 Sunset Blvd. #164
Hollywood, CA. 90046
info@sideshowmediagroup.com

# TABLE OF CONTENTS

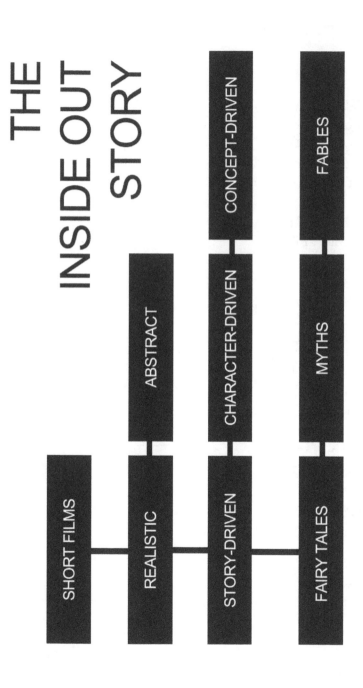

THE
INSIDE OUT
STORY

SHORT FILMS

REALISTIC

ABSTRACT

STORY-DRIVEN

CHARACTER-DRIVEN

CONCEPT-DRIVEN

FAIRY TALES

MYTHS

FABLES

# THANKS

John and Jeremy would like to thank the students of The Los Angeles Film Studies Center for allowing us to workshop hundreds, if not thousands, of short films together. Without all of you and your stories, this book would not be possible.

In addition we wish to thank Chris Krebsbach, who has been such a vital part of all the story development we've experienced.

Thanks also go out to:

Rebecca Ver Straten McSparran, Nathan White, Melanie Hall, Patrick Duff, and Sarah Duff. The Global Short Film Network, Chris DeGarmo, Bushra Shodi, Mike Waid, and Scott Santee.

John would like to thank ...
My wife Katie, for being my love and PIC, Bob & Joan Sanford, Dave Anderson, Dr. Kim Walker, John Bucher, Sr., Cathie Bucher, Matt Bucher, Josh Bucher, Jason Eberly, Tory Nelson, and Jim Krueger. Thanks also to all my friends, especially Peter Burgo, at the C&MA that provided an environment for me to learn the art of storytelling.

Jeremy would like to thank...
My wife Tricia, for her undying love and support through all the years of living with a "never satisfied" writer and filmmaker. Friend, comrade, brother, and fellow writer, Jason Zahodnik - You've always been my biggest fan, and I will always be yours. Cris Cunningham and Tom McCarty (aka the Vacant House team) - So much of what I wrote about in this book, I learned from working with the two of you. Walker Haynes, Chris Easterly, and Dan Braun – 210W. My brother, TJ Maxwell – I hope you find this book to be "adequate." My family, Don and Vicki Casper, Gary Toth, Bret and Jenni Toth, Kamryn and Xander, and Mark and Karen Wilkinson.

# CHAPTER ONE
# INTRODUCTION

## WORKS OF ARCHITECTURE

Having worked with literally thousands of students in the arena of film, we often get asked the same questions. "How can I break into the entertainment industry?" "How can I get my movie made?" "How can I get Hollywood to get on board with what I am doing?" If there were one simple formulaic answer to that question, that's exactly what this book would address. Just once, I wish someone had come up and asked, "How can I make my story better?"

Most people are interested primarily in the end game when it comes to storytelling. They wish for the bright lights of movie premieres, befriending famous actors and having ultimate creative control over their time. Even the most accomplished writers talk of the difficulty they experience in disciplining themselves to write.

While the aspiring rightfully turn to educational training to begin their journey to the big show, they usually are taught all the techniques for creating the feature film of their dreams and then asked to go create a short film. The short film has been a calling card for directors, cinematographers and actors for decades. Unfortunately, the lowly writers of these films rarely have been able to parlay their contribution to the film into anything that resembles career advancement. The reasons why are complex and many. Most short films just aren't that good. This is because there is no agreed upon definition as to what a short film is. Anything that is visually recorded and under 45 minutes in length arguably could be called a short film. While the vast majority of what people call movies or films (even documentary films) have a clear structure, short films are often abstract, slice-of-life character studies and lack any semblance of structure.

So, with such a broad range of running times, can one form of story structure work for all short films? I'm sure many of you have seen plenty of experimental shorts that didn't seem to follow any conventional story structure, but you still walked away from the theatre really liking those films. So, is structure necessary for short films? Do short films follow a different type of structure than feature films? Is it okay for you to go out and just do something CRAZY with a camera and submit it to festivals? The answer to all of these questions is "Yes."

Short films are one of the best mediums for endeavor. With shorts, filmmakers are free to try groundbreaking techniques. If you want to experiment with new methods (whether technical or thematic), go make short films. And, if your highest aspiration is to be an artist who experiments with cinema; working in the film business is not at the top of your priority list; and you are content working out of your home making no-budget films that only handfuls of people will see, then stop reading this book right now and get back to your filmmaking! This book is not for you. However, if you aren't content making short films for the rest of your career; your desire is to ultimately work professionally in the film business; you want to learn techniques that are applicable to good storytelling, no matter what length of film you're making; and you hope to engage audiences who are composed of more than just members of your immediate family and close friends, then keep reading.

Some excellent work has been done to identify structure in story, especially as how it applies to feature film. Joseph Campbell, Robert McKee, John Truby, Chris Vogler, Linda Seger, Blake Snyder and a host of others have made the path clear when it comes to structuring a story that takes place in 90 minutes or more. But when it comes to structure, very little has been stated about short film. Stories and scripts are works of architecture. The short film should be no exception.

While so many filmmakers create short films in an attempt to demonstrate that they can be trusted with longer formats, all that usually is shown is that filmmakers can work with actors and perhaps have some technical prowess. An extremely slim margin of short films demonstrates that filmmakers know how to tell stories. Composing a story is much like composing a tune on a pipe organ. All the keys and pedals (elements of story) are there. Any can be pushed. Many chords can be played. However, just because one can play a single note, or even compose a chord, does not mean that the sound will be pleasant to every ear. In addition, it takes years of mastery to combine chords in succession to create a song. Even more years are required to gain mastery over the sort of songwriting that will touch the hearts of the masses.

So often, we get excited hitting a few notes on the story pipe organ, hearing the sounds that we know we are responsible for making. Once we learn to play a few chords, we often feel we are ready for a concert. Perhaps we should practice and rehearse our storytelling with the same patience and vigor a concert organist employs when creating a piece for public consumption.

What we are doing here is to propose a structure for short-film stories, building on the shoulders of the story giants that have come before us. The short film is an art form unto itself, sharing a relationship with feature film somewhat like the short story shares with the novel. We want to see short films that tell powerful stories. In order to accomplish this, there must be some guidelines. We can't begin to color outside the lines if we cannot even agree that there are any lines to begin with. Short films, like features, should be about story. But, wait, what is that exactly?

## DEFINING STORY

We love stories! We've been inundated with stories for as long as we can remember. In fact, some of us had parents who read stories to us while we were still in the womb. Since the beginning of time, there was never a culture that, in some way, shape or form, didn't use stories to teach, instruct, preserve history, or simply entertain. We can't escape it; the desperate need to tell stories is hardwired into our DNA. We know a good story when we hear one. But, let's take a deep breath, pause for just a second, and ponder one simple question before we hurry out the door with our half-baked script ideas and cameras ready to roll.

## WHAT MAKES A STORY?

It seems simple enough, doesn't it? But, can you stream together a few cleverly chosen words and answer that question with one concise statement? You'd think after all the countless hours of storytelling to which our culture has been exposed, answering that one little question would be a no-brainer.

Well, I've got news for you. Until you're able to succinctly answer that question, you have no business writing stories. And chances are, if you can't answer that question, the stories you've attempted to write up to this point probably meander. They felt more like "chronologies of events" as opposed to well-crafted tales that organically move forward, yet somehow arrive at their satisfying and unpredictable endings. Do your stories seem to fall apart about halfway through? Are you a pro at setting up your story in the beginning, but find you struggle to end your films in a way that doesn't feel cliché or forced?

Does any of this sound familiar? If so, it's time to put on the brakes. Any craftsperson should be able to explain in simple terms what it is they do. And, until a writer is able to do so, their story-writing efforts will continue to be frustrating and the very learnable craft of storytelling will relentlessly elude them.

Flannery O'Connor was once quoted as saying, "I find that most people know what a story is until they sit down to write one." This statement rings true for anyone who has been asked to read the stories of beginning writers. Even some of the most advanced "arrangers of words" have not mastered the art of storytelling. Part of the problem could be that we consider storytelling to be all art and no science - all inspiration and no structure.

Storytelling doesn't necessarily come naturally; it is a craft that cannot be learned by simple exposure. I've been exposed to my fair share of gourmet food; I know good food when I eat it. But, you wouldn't want me to cater your next big event. I'll leave that to the pros. So, why would storytelling, or any other craft for that matter, be different? Do you want to be a haphazard chef in the kitchen of good storytelling, throwing random ingredients together in the hopes that you come up with a satisfactory dish, or do you want to learn how to cook like a gourmet chef and make meals that are complex and tempting to the palette?

John Truby suggests that stories show us the how and why of life. He goes on to say that a story is when a speaker tells a listener what someone did to get what he wanted and why. If storytelling filmmakers even simply followed this model, most short films would immediately improve exponentially. Truby's assertion is loosely based on what has been considered the holy grail of film structure in the United States – Three Act Structure.

Three Act Structure in film first rose to prominence in the observations of scriptwriting guru Syd Field. Field suggested that most cinematic stories featured a first act that consisted of the first 25% of the film. In this first act, we meet the main characters; in particular, our protagonist. We find out that this protagonist wants something or that their normal existence is interrupted in some way. This first act establishes the character(s) of the film. Then there is a second act that consists of the next 50% of the film. In the second act, our protagonist fights for what they want or pursues their goal in some way. There is often a singular force, in the form of an antagonist, that is trying to prevent the protagonist from reaching their goal. This second act establishes the conflict of the story. Finally, we have the third act where our protagonist either achieves or fails to achieve their goal and thus, defeats or is defeated by the antagonist. This is a gross simplification of Three Act Structure, but gives you a basic idea.

Short filmmakers learned the principles of traditional structure and then excused themselves from adhering to it, claiming that there is simply not enough time to tell a Three Act Story in the framework of a short film. But anyone who has ever sat through a short film festival knows that more time is not what short filmmakers need. Some of the longest and most tedious moments of my life have been spent inside a dark theater praying for the end credits of a short film.

Other short filmmakers are hell bent on telling a story where a character only has an internal need or goal and thus, is unable to really make Three Act, or any other structure, work for them. Good films of any length will deal with a character's internal and external NEED, as well as their internal and external GOAL. However, developing all of these concepts in a short film CAN quickly turn it into a feature. In watching short film after short film, we began to notice that films which at least featured an external goal or need were more successful than those that only featured an internal goal or need. Rarely did we see a film that addressed both, but we did see a few and know that it can be done. However, while we saw many films that featured an external need or goal without an internal need or goal, we never saw a short that only addressed an internal need or goal without pursuing an external.

This should not be a revelation. Film is a visual medium and, for years, featured only external needs and goals. The advent of spoken dialogue, and the story complexity that this allowed, really opened up the avenue of exploring what characters needed or desired internally. However, we do not go to the movies to hear characters talk; we go to see them do things. Some films have taken this to an extreme and now only feature action with the thinnest of story to sew it together. This is a mistake as well, as only one emotion can be achieved in this way – excitement.

For the purposes of this book, we will use the following definition of story. A story is:

1. When ONE main character wants or needs something that they pursue. There must be some sort of difficulty in obtaining or achieving this, causing a problem for our protagonist.
2. When that ONE need or goal is achieved, we can SEE it (externally).
3. When there is another force, almost always another character, with the same goal or who is at least in direct opposition to the protagonist achieving that goal (antagonist or contagonist).
4. When the protagonist changes in some way by the story's conclusion.

## THE SHORT FILMMAKERS GREATEST FEAR

I cannot begin to recount how many times I sat with someone helping them craft their story when they confessed the biggest fear they have about their film – that it would be boring. Most filmmakers rightfully have such fear, as most short films ARE boring, but not for the reasons that the film-maker believes. Most short films are boring because they try so hard to be interesting that they end up confusing us and we lose interest. Story analyst Adam Levenberg suggests that beginning storytellers of feature films stick to stories that:

1. Have one hero
2. Take place in the present day United States
3. Take place in contained locations
4. Give the hero a love interest
5. Have some sort of ticking clock
6. Have a clear-cut goal
7. Put life, death, family, or career on the line

When I make similar suggestions to short filmmak-ers, I almost always am met with resistance. "It just sounds boring." Ironically, when asked about their favorite films, the same filmmakers almost always have a few that fit these qualifications.

Many short filmmakers feel these principles are bor-ing because they having a burning concept inside them that doesn't fit within these guidelines well. "I just want to do a sci-fi film." "I want to do something noir – like a period piece." "I can't do that. I want to do a comedy." "I just want to make a film with guns." All these are responses I have heard from budding filmmakers. These storytellers have a concept, but no characters.

This concept-driven approach to story development is how many short filmmakers approach their films, but rarely does this approach yield good stories. To avoid the traps of concept-driven storytelling, we encourage students to begin learning how to tell good **story**-driven stories. In order to craft narratives that are driven by the compelling principles of story, we have to understand our story's main character.

We have to know what makes them tick. We have to understand a bit about their complexities.

An old adage of the storytelling world is "simple stories and complex characters." Many beginning storytellers fear that their plotlines are not complex enough and people will find them boring. Many of these same filmmakers will have paper-thin characters explaining the plot of the film to each other. Audiences are much more intrigued by a deeply complex character that reminds them of themselves or someone they know. There is a sea of short films out there that lose their audience in the first minute or two of the film because of the complexity of the story they are telling. Making your audience feel smart because they understand the story is always a winning formula. Making your audience feel emotion because they relate to the complexity of the character is doubly effective.

Finally, let us offer a quick word about genre. Many storytellers automatically think dramas when you talk about structure. The truth is structure applies to genres across the board. Comedies, horror films and sci-fi thrillers all benefit from the same guidelines of structure. Well-developed characters are not specific to the dramatic genre. Character-driven films are not necessarily dramas. High-concept comedies with character-driven plot lines are almost consistently successful at the box office. And character-driven plot lines are almost impossible to achieve without structure.

Short films are a unique medium. Have you ever seen a short film that felt like a two-hour film crammed into ten minutes? Unfortunately we have too. This is one of the biggest mistakes short filmmakers make; it's a tried-and-true recipe for disaster. Short films shouldn't be JUST for the feature filmmaker wannabes. Shorts are definitely a unique medium and there is no such thing as a "one-size-fits-all" training that works across the board for both features and shorts. Writing abridged features is NOT what this book is about. Though many of the principles we explore are pulled directly from the world of feature writing, our goal is to show you how to apply these principles to the unique medium of short film.

So, where do we go from here? We've asked the question, "What makes a story?" We've started talking about different types of short films. We've looked at various formats and why many of these formats don't work well for the short filmmaker. And we've set the stage for a new look at how to approach short filmmaking.

So, which type of short film are we going to discuss? If we included every single kind of short film, this book would be exhaustive… and exhausting. In order to facilitate discussion, we've broken short films down into several tiers. We'll begin by putting short films into two primary categories: Abstract Films and Realism Films. Abstract films are not the primary focus of this book, but due to their relevance and importance in the short-film world, we will spend a chapter looking at the two major categories of Abstract Films: The Experimental Film and the Thematic Abstract Film.

Next, we'll look at the Realism Short film and its three subcategories: the Character-Driven Short Film, the Concept-Driven Short Film and the Story-Driven Short Film. Then we will spend three chapters breaking down the Story-Driven Short film into its three categories: The Fable, The Fairytale and The American Myth. In the final chapters of the book, we will cover specific structure for short films, how to develop a story from a character, and the next step for the filmmaker after reading this book.

So what is The Inside Out Story? The Inside Out Story is a way of identifying the bare essentials of different types of stories by turning them inside-out. The Inside Out Story refers to the relationship between two major components of the main character in a story. Every well-developed, main character has two goals - an interior goal and an exterior goal (inside out). If you are able to clearly establish these two goals, take your character on a journey that, despite great adversity, ultimately leads them to accomplish these goals, then you are already leagues ahead of most filmmakers who ramble on, page after page, with no clear direction.

With commitment and practice, anyone can learn the techniques of crafting great stories. So, let's get started.

# CHAPTER TWO
# ABSTRACT SHORT FILMS

As we discussed in the opening chapter, we have been inundated with films since we were born. We know, by nature, whether or not a story works and the universal reasons we like those films are obvious – the boy gets the girl, the bad guy is defeated or we experience an adventure we could never experience in real life.

Documentarian Ken Burns said that a good story is "1+1=3." What a great way to look at storytelling. No matter how many books one reads on storytelling or how many beat structures one memorizes, in the end, a good story is never the sum of all of its parts – it's so much more. In the world of storytelling, something magical should happen when we add 1 and 1 together.

Have you ever left the theatre loving the film you just saw, but you couldn't quite articulate why? Somewhere imbedded in your bewilderment was that elusive digit - that extra "1." If we, the authors, had the power to unveil the mystical part of the universe from where that extra digit originated, we'd be writing a very different book… and we'd be two very rich dudes!

At the end of every writing seminar, I tell my students that, when constructing good stories, at some point the unexplainable artistry of writing must enter the picture and like all inconceivable things, we tend to spiritualize what we do not understand. There IS an incomprehensible, spiritual factor to storytelling that eludes even the greatest writers. Some people have a gift for discovering those moments. Some writers have developed the ability to do so through years and years of tireless training and experience. And, the more one learns about storytelling, the more one discovers how incredibly deep the oceans of story theory are. As is the case in any discipline, the more you learn, the more you realize how little you know. For every theory you comprehend, you'll discover a thousand more corridors just waiting to be explored.

One of our main objectives in writing this book is to demystify the *entry* process of writing the short film. Many of you have already tried your hand at short filmmaking and have discovered that constructing films that give audiences that magical extra "1," and do so in a quick five minutes, are very difficult films to create.

For the purposes of better understanding short films and for ease of discussion, we are going to sort short films into two major groups: the *Realism* short film and the *Abstract* short film. Nearly all short films can be placed into one of these two exhaustively broad categories. And, although understanding the differences between these two types of films is relatively easy, it's important that we make the distinction between these two groups early in our discussion. Knowing into which category your story falls automatically narrows your focus as you begin to write your script. All of the reading that follows hinges on understanding into which of these two groups your film fall.

During our story workshop sessions, we ask students to bring story ideas to the classroom for discussion. The multifaceted purpose of the exercise is to get our student writers accustomed to working in collaboration with other writers, to assess the story problems within a group situation and to receive suggestions on how to make their stories stronger. One of the main issues we run into during these pitch sessions is students who create stories in which their main characters do not have clear **external goals**. We will discuss the "external goals" of main characters in much more detail in coming chapters. Without clear external goals, stories have no direction; in fact, they really aren't stories at all; they're just scenarios.

Students who try to write films without character goals are often very lost; they can't figure out where to go with their stories; they just seem to be wandering around in writing circles. The reason for their frustration is simple; if a writer doesn't determine the main external goal of the lead character, the author has no idea where the story is going. The story literally could go in a million random directions. And when a writer is looking at the prospect of a million different ideas, the task of writing starts to become quite overwhelming.

When we hold workshop sessions with students and try to discuss stories that don't have characters with clear goals, the brainstorming sessions are quite fruitless. The group loses focus and the sessions devolve into a bunch of people throwing out one wild, off-the-wall suggestion after another and in every situation, we nearly always stop the session and tell the writer to go back to the drawing board and figure out their main character's external goal. In order for writing to be productive, authors must learn how to limit their options. Writing becomes so much easier once you know *exactly* what your main character is trying to *do* in the story and what *type* (genre) of story you're trying to tell.

If you're writing a horror story, there are certain rules you must follow. If you're writing a romantic comedy, there are laws of the rom-com universe that simply can't be broken. Artists never like to be put into boxes, but good writers understand that learning the rules of a medium can actually be quite freeing. Learning what "kind" of film you're trying to make and learning the subsequent guidelines for that type of film will actually spark creativity and open doors of possibility. One of the main purposes of this book is not to tell you exactly how to write short films, but rather to help you narrow your gaze and avoid distractions. If you're writing a

pure horror film, then get the rules of romantic comedy off
the table so you aren't distracted; if your story fits into the
*fable* category, keep your story simple and don't try to tell a
*myth* or a *fairy tale*.

You'd be surprised at how many of our students
have no idea what genre of film they're writing, even after
they've pitched their entire story to us in class! So, to begin
to understand what kind of film you're creating, first ask the
question, "Am I making a *realistic* short film or an *abstract*
short film?" As stated above, these two categories are in-
sanely broad; thousands of different types of films could fit
into these two categories. But, understanding the differences
between *abstract* and *realism* and knowing into which category your film falls is the first step in the process of narrowing
your focus in order to improve your writing.

There is one final thing we want to address before we
begin to dissect these two categories. As stated in the intro
chapter, we have designed this book to help anyone who
wants to make short films, but one main target audience is
those filmmakers who want to parlay their short filmmaking into full-blown feature filmmaking careers. You may not
have any ideas for short films stirring around in your brain
at this particular moment, and that's okay; this book still
can be highly beneficial for those who are just exploring the
world of short filmmaking. By learning about these two categories (and all of the subsequent categories), filmmakers can
determine on which arena of short filmmaking they should
be focused. The filmmaker who is only concerned about
screening their films at art houses and on the festival circuit
will, more than likely focus on creating a very different type
of short film than the filmmaker who is focused on creating
short form stories for use on the Internet, or the filmmakers
whose future goal is to direct features in the Hollywood
studio system. Not only do we hope to narrow the focus of
the writer to help them create better stories, we also desire to

help filmmakers decide where they should be focusing their short-film efforts, based on their career goals.

So, let's talk about abstract films. What makes an abstract film? By definition, an abstract film seeks to defy... definition. To try to come up with a model for creating abstract films would be pointless and counterproductive. A certain devil-may-care spirit is crucial to the creation of abstract films. The purpose of the abstract film is to push boundaries, stir emotion, provide experiences and express the intangible feelings of the artist. The abstract film is the one type of film that truly exists for art's sake. We had to teach story structure for years, incessantly pushing the virtues of three-act structure before we finally conceded that there are some really great short films out there that just break all the rules.

Does this mean that abstract films are beyond deconstruction? By no means! In fact, the abstract film begs to be whittled down to its finer parts – to uncover, in some cases, a deeper meaning that the filmmaker was trying to convey.

So, how then do we classify the abstract film?

Any film that is NOT "realistic" *can* be an abstract film.

And, any realistic short film *can have* abstract elements in it.

How's that for a definition? Although many abstract films lack the conventional structure of the Hollywood Three-Act story, many abstract films still have hidden beneath their surfaces semblances of some type of structure that holds the cinematic experience together. Filmmakers who make good abstract films (and by "good," we mean films that tend to resonate with more people than just the filmmakers and their moms) tend to be more focused on the structure of their films than audiences might realize at first glance.

Abstract films exist to serve a variety of purposes. They can be personal expressions of the artist, showcase specific film techniques, explore emotions, etc.

In the intro chapter we talked briefly about "why" we want to make films. It is our assumption that those of you who are reading this book want your films to be seen by people... LOTS of people. Unless you desire to work in a vacuum, at some point, if you want your work to be seen, understood or experienced by living, breathing human beings, it is necessary for you to take your audience into consideration when creating your films, even when making abstract ones.

## THE EXPERIMENTAL FILM

One of the most practical and basic purposes of the abstract film is to experiment – to create a springboard for the discussion of cinematic technique. Ground-breaking film techniques most often are birthed in short films that are created by some filmmaker who simply had a vision for the medium of cinema and wanted to see what could be done when he or she pushed the camera to its limits.

Here's how the progression usually unfolds. A filmmaker tries an experiment by playing with lighting, frame rates, exposures, and movement. The resulting effect is uncommon, edgy, peculiar, but if successful, it's eye catching and we want to see more. This newly discovered technique typically finds its way into the world of advertising and after a few years, we eventually see that technique in all of its fully funded, multi-million-dollar glory at multiplex theatres across the globe. Many of those groundbreaking techniques were birthed in some filmmaker's small studio or backyard shed. This progression to the big-screen, however, is usually a long process (sometimes taking years or decades) and rarely experienced by the filmmaker who created the technique.

The movie, *The Matrix* (1999), was lauded for pioneering the now- trademarked technique called Bullet Photography. In the opening sequence of the film, the character of Trinity, played by Carrie-Anne Moss, is hotly pursued by agents in the dreamlike world of *The Matrix*. In a moment that wowed audiences and set the stage for one amazing, eye-popping effect after another, Trinity leaps from the ground and freezes in time as the camera continues to dolly around her. The common moviegoer thought the moment was really cool, but filmmakers in the audience wet their pants. We saw something impossible - ramped slow motion, freeze frames, and camera movements all happening simultaneously. The Wachowski siblings had discovered a never-before-seen camera trick!

But, nothing could be further from the truth. Directors Andy and Lana Wachowski and Director of Photography Bill Pope certainly deserve credit for perfecting the technique, but the very first application of what we now call Bullet Photography occurred before the motion picture camera was even created. In 1872, photographer Eadweard Muybridge was hired to settle a debate. The former governor of California and race-horse owner Leland Sanford wanted to know if there was ever a moment in time when all four hooves of a horse were simultaneously off the ground during a full gallop. He asked Muybridge to find the answer.

And so, over one hundred years before Neo and Trinity rescued humanity from Agent Smith and the mind-numbing world of *The Matrix*, Muybridge ventured out to the racetrack, lined up a series of cameras rigged to take a single photograph as a horse named Occidental galloped by. The result was a progression of photographs that, when watched in succession, created the illusion of movement - a series of frames, each created by a solitary camera. *The Horse in Motion* (1872) was an experimental film that not only introduced us to the most basic theories of motion-picture technique, but also served as a starting point for the creation of a mind-blowing effect that is still widely used in action films today.

The idea of using multiple cameras to create motion lay dormant for over a hundred years before it was reintroduced. In 1985, German heavy-metal band *Accept* reintroduced Muybridge's technique in a music video for their song *Midnight Mover*. The video features several moments where the camera rapidly dollies around members of the band as they play their instruments. The effect is dizzying and far from perfect. But, the technique elaborated on Muybridge's experiment by introducing dramatic camera moves when the images were played together.

And finally, in 1999, moviegoers witnessed the greatest use of the technique to date. Fully realized, with all of the kinks worked out – *The Matrix* cemented its place in cinematic history for its use of a "never-before-seen" technique.

So, despite our incessant push for students to adhere to story structure and learn the rules of fables, fairy tales, and myths, it's important to note that all great advances in the world of filmmaking were birthed by some filmmaker who looked at the inner workings of a camera and dared to ask the question, "What if?" We need filmmakers who are willing to do that and if that's you, by all means, go out there and push the limits of filmmaking to their breaking points. But understand, in choosing such a path, you're limiting the world of cinema in which you will likely be able to work. We'll discuss that in more detail later on.

## THE THEMATIC ABSTRACT FILM

Pushing cinematic technique is not the only purpose that abstract films serve. Abstract films not only can push the boundaries of technology, but they also can push the boundaries of theme and structure. Thematic abstract films explore narrative and cinematic *concepts*, whereas realistic films tackle the specific issues of *story* and *character*. The line between abstract and realism is gray. Abstract films *can* have characters and realistic films *can* have abstract elements, but for the purpose of our discussion, if a film has a **story** (a human character trying to solve a human problem) or it seeks to explore the humanity of a particular **character** (the character-driven short film), no matter how abstract the visuals may be, we will classify that film as a realistic short film.

As stated above, abstract films are a great medium in which artists can explore broad, general themes without the use of story. Try this exercise. Take a few minutes and make a list of objects that most people associate with the word "anger." Now, imagine if you were to film each of those objects (being mindful of angles and lighting) and edit them together in a fashion that evoked the feeling of the word. You add some music to your film, enter it into some festivals and screen it for some audiences. Fantastic! You're a filmmaker! But, you haven't made a realistic short film or in other words, you haven't developed a character or a story. This doesn't mean your film doesn't have artistic merit; films like this can be beautiful, moving and thought provoking; it takes a very skillful filmmaker to connect with audiences solely through the creation of mood and feeling without the use of story, but films like this do not tell stories.

Imagine if you saw a montage of the following images: a red rose, Cupid firing his arrow, a couple kissing, lit candles sitting on a table for two and a silhouette of a man and woman walking down the beach. You don't need any story to know that this is a montage exploring the theme of "love." Now imagine if you saw a different montage with these images: a cracked whiskey bottle, a catfish covered in mud, a rocket lifting off a launch pad, a smiling African boy, and a pack of cigarettes. What theme is being explored in this montage? What if I told you that it, too, is exploring the

theme of love? Every image in that last montage is something from my own personal life that represents love to me.

Is there anything wrong with my montage? Not at
all. I made my montage for art's sake; I didn't make it to
win awards; I just wanted to put into images what my fee-
ble words could not express. And, there's a chance that if I
edit my images together in a provoking manner, a *handful* of
other people who have shared similar life experiences might
resonate with my montage as well. But, therein lies the biggest challenge abstract filmmakers face. Many abstract filmmakers fail to recognize that what resonates with them does
not necessarily resonate with everyone else, which is often
why many audiences walk away from abstract films scratch-
ing their heads and uttering to themselves, "Huh?"

Some artists do not care how people react to their
art, but for most filmmakers, "Huh?" is not the reaction we
desire when our credits roll. I've seen far too many abstract
films that come off as comical and pretentious because the
filmmaker failed to speak in a language the audience could
understand. We have an impolite phrase for this type of
filmmaking. We call it cinematic masturbation. It's a type of
filmmaking that only the filmmaker really gets to enjoy.

The challenge for the abstract filmmaker is to avoid
clichés (like red roses and Cupid firing an arrow), but at
the same time still connect with audiences. The artistry of
abstract filmmaking lies primarily in a filmmaker's understanding of the language of cinema. It is impossible to discuss any aspect of *abstract* or *realistic* filmmaking (from writing, acting, directing, cinematography, editing, etc.) without
discussing the language of cinema. Language of cinema
deals primarily the audiences' relationship with the visual
image and the filmmaker's understanding of (and ability to
exploit) that relationship.

For example, looking at the second montage above,
what happens when audiences see an image of a catfish

covered in mud followed by an image of a rocket lifting off a launch pad? The juxtaposition of those two images forces audiences to find a relationship between the two images and deduce meaning from that. As unconnected as a catfish and rocket seem, if I put those two images up on the screen next to each other, audiences WILL have a reaction to it. They will FIND meaning in their contrast, even if no intended meaning existed. And that meaning would change if the images were shot in close up or in wide shots or if they were lit at night or during the day or shot in slow or fast motion, etc. The combination of all these elements affects how audiences understand the images.

But, the skilled filmmaker doesn't randomly choose images or camera angles. They carefully select their shots and use juxtaposition to create *intended* meaning while incorporating lighting, camera angles, editing and sound to further guide their audiences to a desired, specific emotional conclusion. This is all language of cinema.

So, good abstract filmmakers should be mindful of the following three things:

1. Good abstract films have *themes*.
2. Abstract filmmaking is about the informed execution of the *language of cinema*.
3. Abstract filmmakers have an *awareness of their audience*.

*Pan with Us* is a gorgeous, animated short film created by award-winning filmmaker, David Russo. At first glance, it would be easy to say that *Pan with Us* is purely experimental. Russo's use of animated images in the real world is unlike anything most of us have seen. But, by incorporating the prose of Robert Frost's poem of the same name, Russo elevates his film above the threshold of mere experiment and creates something more – a thematic abstract. When engag-

ing *Pan with Us*, one doesn't focus only on the technique –
the animation experiment Russo seems to be conducting – it
also makes us feel something. Russo's film yearned to do
more than just look interesting; it had a theme.

Language of cinema will come up often in the following chapters, but an exhaustive study of its disciplines
deserves a full library of books and will not be our primary
focus.

Keep in mind that theme is different from genre.
Genre is story based; in other words, you can't have genre
without characters and drama. If you want to make an abstract film that explores the theme of terror, you might bor-
row heavily from techniques used in horror films, but your
film is not technically a horror film because it doesn't tell a
story. Instead, your film is an abstract film that seeks to incite
the *mood* or *feeling* of terror through the use of language of
cinema. This is one of the reasons why realistic filmmakers
should not ignore abstract filmmaking. Imagine a filmmaker
who has mastered the technique of creating the feeling of terror *just* through the use of images, lighting, music, etc. Now
image if that filmmaker applied the same techniques to a
film with characters and a story. The best films use elements
of all disciplines.

So, how long should your abstract film be? Audiences need a good reason to stay in their seats when they go to
movie theatres. History proves that audiences engage films
for a extended periods of time, IF they are given stories.
Without story, audiences lose interest in the subject matter
quickly. There's a reason we can binge watch shows like
*Breaking Bad* for days on end, or we can sit through eleven
hours of *Lord of the Rings* and not think twice; it's because
we are riveted by the elements of story – characters trying to
solve problems.

If your film lacks this very basic element of storytelling, then you dramatically reduce the amount of time your audience will remain engaged with your film.

Experimental abstract films that explore a new, fascinating film technique are captivating for a couple of minutes. Thematic Abstract Films might be able to take us on longer journeys of four to five minutes by engaging us with their riveting montages, artistic imagery and beautiful music, but if too much time passes, eventually your audiences will start asking the question, "So… what happens next?" And what your audiences are really asking is, "So… where's the story?"

This is why pure abstract films do not make great feature films. Even surreal filmmakers like Ingmar Bergman, Krzysztof Kieslowski, and Terrence Malick know that to engage their audiences for extended amounts of time, they must have some semblance of a narrative story, even if it's ever so faint, to keep audiences in their seats for more than a few minutes.

Every student of film should be required to make at least one abstract film. Challenge yourself; are you able to incite a specific emotional response in an audience through a film that does not incorporate any form of story? Are there particular themes to which you are drawn in your filmmaking? Try this exercise: Pick a theme that's close to you and see if you can make a film that relies solely on the use of imagery and editing to convey that theme. The techniques that you discover will help you when it comes time to incorporate that same theme into a short film with an actual narrative.

If you don't have the resources to shoot an abstract film, select a theme and then scour the Internet for images that convey your theme. Print them out and create a mosaic of images or import your images into editing software and cut them together with music. Once completed, ask yourself the following questions: What do your images have in common? How would the feeling or mood of your piece change if you rearranged the order of the images? What types of images did you avoid? Did you use any unconventional film techniques to help convey the mood?

The things you learn from this exercise will inform your future films.

The medium of film can be so much more than just a "record of drama." It can take audiences to the heights and depths of human emotion through the use of simple pictures or incomprehensibly complex images. It is the filmmaker who speaks this language fluently, whose work stands out above the rest.

# CHAPTER THREE
# REALISM SHORT FILMS

*Character Driven vs. Concept Driven vs. Story Driven*

Now that we've taken a 30,000-foot look at story structure by examining the Abstract short film, let's decelerate, lower our altitude and bring the story plane in for a closer look at our narrative surroundings.

As we discussed in the previous chapter, short films can generally be placed in one of two categories – Abstract and Realism. For the most part, abstract films tend to be the stuff of art, made by filmmakers who simply want to explore the medium of film to see how far they can push the boundaries. Although this is a beneficial endeavor, most filmmakers will not be handed the keys to the gates of Hollywood by only making purely abstract films. In the last chapter of this book, we will discuss in detail the various paths filmmakers take to achieve success in the entertainment business by looking at all the different types of short films they can make. Generally speaking, abstract films are not conducive to launching a career in Hollywood.

So, let's shift gears. In this chapter, we want to move our gaze from the abstract film and examine in more detail short films that fall into the "Realism" category.

What do we mean when we say a film is "realistic?" For the purposes of this discussion, realistic short films will be defined as films that rely predominantly on well-defined characters and/or sequences of events that take place in a defined universe. We are moving out of the realm of the esoteric and into the world of the concrete.

Realism short films exist in reality. That reality might

be the fantasy world of Middle Earth, or a "...galaxy far, far away," but the worlds are "real" nonetheless. Reality in films simply means the story has characters who are subject to certain clearly defined rules of a particular universe. That universe can be anything that you as the writer envision - fantastical, spiritual, scientific or horrific. But, the number one rule of the realistic short film is that your story world must have rules and those rules must be obeyed.

This is one of the reasons why we encourage our students to avoid telling stories that take place in some- one's mind. If you decide to delve into the subconscious of a character, you are immediately moving into the world of the abstract. In the ill-defined world of the subconscious, it can be tempting for writers to throw the rules of their universe out the window, go crazy with their storytelling and confuse audiences. It also typically leads to very lazy writing.

Filmgoers, believe it or not, prefer movies that ad- here to limits. When I go to the theatre to watch a horror/ drama movie about a boy who "sees dead people," I expect the filmmaker to adhere to the rules of those two genres. If, while viewing the movie, *The Sixth Sense* (1999), Bruce Willis spontaneously broke out into a song and dance in the mid- dle of the film, I would feel cheated as an audience member (even if Willis is a phenomenal singer and dancer – I have no observational experience on the matter). "Singing and danc- ing" does not follow the rules of the horror/drama genre. I long for filmmakers to play within the confines of the genre playground that (s)he established during the setup of their film. (We will discuss this in more detail in the American Myth chapter.)

Could *The Sixth Sense* work as a horror/drama/mu- sical? You bet! But in order for that to work, the filmmaker would need to have a song and dance number within the first five minutes of the movie (to alert the audience to the type of film they're about to watch) and then subject themselves to the rules of musicals (as well as horror and drama). As you can see in this simple example, the more genres you try to combine, the more rules you have to follow.

Combining genres is the stuff Hollywood is made of. More combined genres means broader demographics, which means more ticket sales. But, regardless of the monetary benefits, combining genres often produces some of the most fascinating pieces of work. More than likely, your favorite movies are the combination of several genres. James Cameron successfully combined the genres of drama, action, romance, disaster and even horror in his movie, *Titanic* (1997). No wonder audiences for that film were so broad, consisting of everyone from fifteen-year-old boys to sixty-five-year-old women – two demographics that historically never watch the same movies.

So, to reiterate, if you've decided to work in the realm of realistic short films, the very first rule you must follow is that your story must take place in a clearly defined reality. Keep in mind that if your reality is obscure or different from present day reality, then you are required to explain the rules of the universe to your audience and you must do so clearly and very early on in the narrative. This is one of the reasons why historic films, fantasy films and sci-fi films are difficult (but not impossible) to do in short films. They require a certain level of grandiosity and explanation of the world in order for the stories to work. *The Fellowship of the Ring* (2001) opened with a brilliantly constructed prologue that lasted a full ten minutes (a short film in itself); the world was so huge that we needed a vast amount of information before we could even begin to engage in the story. Explaining the rules of a universe takes time – a luxury short filmmakers don't have.

Almost every sci-fi or fantasy film our students make inevitably requires a text-driven prologue at the beginning of the film similar to the opening scroll at the start of every *Star*

*Wars* film. This isn't necessarily "good" filmmaking, but the text-driven prologue is a device that can help disseminate a LOT of information very quickly.

Early on in the movie *The Village* (2004), writer/director M. Night Shyamalan gave the audiences the rules of *The Village* universe through exposition (through dialogue, a character literally stated the rules that the characters must follow).

1. Let the bad color not be seen. It attracts them.
2. Never enter the woods. That is where they wait.
3. Heed the warning bell for they are coming.
4. One man should hold post in the tower each night.
5. The safe color should be worn upon approaching the forbidden line.

Is this filmmaking at its best? Arguably not. But, regardless, the audience understood the rules and they served as an excellent device that Shyamalan used to create suspense. As we watch the film, we now know that when we hear the warning bell, "they" are coming. The bell, without the rules, would just be a bell. Shyamalan does a masterly job of adhering to the rules of this universe throughout the course of the film. He established his boundaries and played within his pre-determined confines. (There was no singing and dancing in *The Village*.)

In the skillfully constructed genre film, *Reign of Fire* (2002), director Rob Bowman used a similar technique to create suspense. In the film, British refugees, fighting desperately to preserve their lives from the apocalyptic onslaught of fire-breathing dragons, quoted the rules of their society like a mantra:

1. **What do we do when we are awake?**
   *Keep two eyes on the sky.*

2.  **What do we do when we sleep?**
    *Keep one eye on the sky.*
3.  **What do we do when we see them?**
    *Dig hard, dig deep, go for shelter and never look back.*

Vague rules, but eerie and suspenseful, nonetheless. Even if we never saw a single dragon in the film, we know that our main characters are facing a very threatening and dangerous adversary. Just watching a character sleep in *Reign of Fire* sets audiences on edge.

The only time breaking the rules of a story universe works is when the overall purpose of the story is to challenge a rule. For example, in Walt Disney's *The Little Mermaid* (1989), the primary rule of the ocean is that merpeople cannot interact with humans. The narrative conflict of *The Little Mermaid* hinges upon the challenging of this rule. Shakespeare's *Romeo and Juliet* follows the same model – warring families cannot be friends. Both stories challenge societal norms in their own, unique way.

In the movie, *The Silence of the Lambs* (1991), Jodie Foster's character breaks every rule given to her. She was told not to "go near the glass" or take anything from Dr. Lecter, or tell him personal details about her life. She breaks every rule, but the filmmakers address her rebellion by showing how she suffers the consequences – the incompletion of her internal journey (a consequence that was intentionally and masterfully executed).

Now that we've looked at some of the basic ground rules of realistic films, let's lower our story plane just a few more thousand feet and dissect the realistic short film into its smaller parts.

Realistic short films tend to fall into three clearly defined categories:

1.  The character-driven short film
2.  The concept-driven short film
3.  The story-driven short film

In most of the chapter entitled, "The American Myth," we will examine the story-driven short film, so let's take a look at the first two types of realistic short films.

Though many examples from feature films will still be used, it's important to note that, at this point in the discussion, we will look more closely at short films and what makes them unique and "set apart" from features.

## THE CHARACTER-DRIVEN SHORT FILM

Like abstract films, the character-driven film is a type that works well in shorts. The short-film medium seems to be tailor made for these two types of films. The most important reason is that these types of films just work better in a short time frame. It is seldom that you will see a feature-length, abstract film in your local multiplex; the Terrence Malicks of the world are few and far between.

Malick's film, *The Tree of Life* (2011), is a rare example of an abstract feature film that had (some) mainstream appeal. But even this film relied heavily on A-list actors and a loose, character-driven narrative (realism) to stitch its disparate parts together and consequently, *The Tree of Life* (just like a short abstract film) was highly polarizing – audiences either loved it or thought it was a pretentious, self-indulgent waste of film. Do you care if your films are highly polarizing? If your goal is to make a career out of filmmaking, you should. Hollywood wants to see that you can reach the greatest number of people – abstract films don't do that.

So what is a character-driven short film? A character-driven story is a narrative that exists primarily for the purpose of exploring a particular moment in the life of a character. You will often hear these stories referred to as slice-of-life or day-in-the-life films. There is typically no strong, overarching external goal in the story – though, as we will see in the following case studies, even character-driven stories work best when there is *some* goal, even if it is subtle. The main character isn't necessarily trying to achieve any-thing or solve a problem (which are the basic elements of the story-driven short film). In a character-driven short film, we simply watch a character live out their life over the course of a set amount of time.

The fun thing about the character-driven film is the fact that there is a lot of freedom to explore and play; there aren't a lot of rules. The ultimate goal is to simply make a film that explores the life of a deeply fascinating character. But, before you start pounding out your character-driven, short film opus, there are a few things you should consider. Though character-driven films can work effectively without the type of story structure we will discuss in future chapters, there are ways to make your character-driven films better (and more appealing to a broader audience… and to Holly-wood).

Many of our students want to make what they think are character-driven stories. For whatever reason, they are drawn to copious amounts of dialogue – characters sitting around in apartments or coffee shops pontificating about life. Which, ironically, is the exact opposite of what the medium of film does effectively. Film is a medium of action. Good film stories should be about what characters DO in a physical world, not about what they say. Dialogue has its place in film, but it should serve to underscore the actions of your characters. Films that are primarily driven by dialogue are not necessarily bad, but they are not using the medium of film to its fullest.

With that said, however, the character-driven film tends to rely more heavily on dialogue than other types of films. This is not a requirement, but it's something about which filmmaker should be aware. Great dialogue doesn't automatically make great films. It's up to you to find ways of making dialogue scenes more interesting and visually appealing.

When constructing a character-driven short film, the first thing with which you want to begin is, obviously... the character. And for the character-driven short film, a couple paragraphs of information about your hero isn't enough. You want to create an in depth character with a rich history and multiple layers. In other words, you want to *create a character that has a truly unique perspective on the world.*

Many writing gurus will tell you to "write what you know," but many of us, on the surface, are pretty average people; there might not be much about our humdrum lives that seems worthy of cinematic exploration. What I've discovered, however in working with the college-age set is that everyone, no matter how old or young, has some aspect of their inner lives that is uniquely "them" – something about their life journey that is profoundly fascinating. It is in this "uniquely you" internal place that you will find great fodder for the creation of compelling characters.

If you're unsure what part of you is unique, ask yourself this question, "What are my greatest fears?" A grad school professor once told me that I wouldn't write anything worth reading unless I was writing absolutely terrified. To write something with substance, you must be willing to expose the darker parts of your inner self. For the young writer, this type of vulnerability is difficult; many youthful writers simply aren't mature enough to engage truthfully in that type of emotional exposure. It isn't a necessity to write from this place, but from this place, deep, resonate honesty can emerge. Audiences can sniff out stories and characters that have been forced – they reek of formulas and immaturity. But narratives created from a place of experience feel authentic. We tell our students to write about what they've experienced, not about what they've been taught. Keep in mind that writing from this place of fear is not a genre-specific endeavor; even comedies tend to come from places of deep pain.

There is something within every single person reading this book that can serve as the foundation of a deeply interesting character; now it's your job to identify that "something" and externalize it. Make it a living, breathing person. The externalization of internal conflict is one of the primary jobs of filmmakers. Unlike novel writers, we filmmakers don't get to spend exorbitant amounts of time telling our audiences what a character is feeling. Instead, we must find ways to reveal what's going on inside our characters by giving them actions that reveal how they feel internally– externalizing internal conflict. For example, I can tell the audience through dialogue or voice over that my main character has trouble forgiving (this is bad filmmaking), or I can put my character into a situation that forces my character to display for the audience his inability to forgive. Follow the old adage – show; don't tell.

Even though character-driven stories tend to be more open ended when it comes to structure, the best stories, regardless of which subcategory of realism into which they fall, have some semblance of structure.

In the George Hickenlooper-directed and Billy Bob Thornton-written short film, *Some Folks Call It a Sling Blade,* and in Jared Hess', *Peluca,* we find perfect examples of the character-driven short film. Both of these films were created primarily to explore deeply fascinating main characters. We don't need much story. It is not imperative in the character-driven short film for main characters to have *strong*, overarching external goals. Many other story elements that we typically find in Hollywood films may or may not be present in the character-driven short film.

When writing the character-driven film, you want to start by creating a character unlike anyone we've seen previously. We go to the movies to experience realities other than our own, so start by creating the most fascinating character you possibly can. Karl is not your run-of-the-mill, average Joe that we typically see walking down the street; if he were, no one would have taken notice of *Some Folks Call It a Sling Blade*.

Everything about Karl's outward presentation to the world is fascinating and unlike anything we've seen before - everything from the clothes he wears, to the way he walks down the hallway, to the awkward cadences of his speech, to his stance and his body position. We are riveted by the external presentation of his character. Nearly the exact same thing could be said about Jon Heder's character Seth in *Peluca*. Both characters are, in a vulgar sense, train wrecks – we just can't take our eyes off them.

On the most basic and prejudicial level, we make assessments of people based on how they present themselves to the world (whether their presentation is done so consciously or not). I tell my coworkers something about myself by the way I dress. Do I "dress for success," or am I a "jeans and t-shirt" kind of guy? Are my clothes too big or too small for my frame? Do I only wear black? Are my clothes too youthful for my age, or do I dress like my grandpa? Or does my attire suggest that I really don't care at all about how I look?

These are not just clothing concerns that you want to leave up to your costume designer once you're in production. As a writer, you need to consider everything that potentially tells us something about the character you're presenting.

## DEVELOPING A CHARACTER

As stated earlier, your description and understanding of your character should be deep, layered and well thought out. Next, we are going to take a look at some basic questions you can ask yourself as you endeavor to construct a fascinating main character. There are **Six Crucial Character Questions** you should ask about your character when coming up with your story. We will look at the first four of the six questions in the following section. But before we look at these questions, it's important to note that there is a big difference between creating a character that's interesting and creating a character that's primed and ready to go on a story journey. Sometimes the most fascinating characters to watch (characters that might work well in a character-driven short film) might not make strong characters in a story-driven film. In the story-driven story section of this chapter, we will answer the final two questions from our list of Six Crucial Character Questions – two questions that must be answered before you send your character off on the story journey.

So as you begin constructing your character, start off by answering the first four of our six questions. Experiment! Push things to their limits and see where it takes you. Have fun as you develop your character.

**1. What does your character spend most of his or her time doing?**

For the adult character, this most often is going to be their profession. What we do for a living (whether we're happy about our job or not) defines us. If your main character is a child, the thing that preoccupies their day could be anything from school to hobbies to keeping the peace between feuding parents. How we spend our days says something about who we are. At first glance, this might seem like a trivial question to answer, but you'd be amazed at how many stories are about a person whose occupation puts them at serious odds with the world around them.

**2. What is my character's Age/Race/Gender/Sexual Orientation/Socioeconomic Status/Religion?**
Although these elements seem obvious, it's important to fully and intentionally answer them. In a well-constructed, character-driven film, these elements serve as crucial building blocks for your story. The story you would tell about a 7-year-old, Asian girl who aspires to become a ballerina who comes from a wealthy Buddhist family should be markedly different from a story you tell about a 45-year-old, Caucasian, urban, gay male who comes from an atheist background and delivers pizzas for a living. As you can see, just by quickly defining these simple qualities, I'm starting to define the parameters of a person and create well-rounded characters who are interesting. When constructing your story, ask yourself, "What happens if I change one of these elements?" What happens if I make our first character a 65-year-old woman instead of a 7-year-old child? Do my story possibilities and character dynamic dramatically change? If not, then I'm not allowing my character to drive the narrative.

The following two questions are two of the most important ones you can ask when creating your characters. It's important for us to spend some time reflecting on these questions, since we will be building on them in future chapters.

**3. What is your character's "normal" world?**
When we refer to the "normal world" of your character, we're actually talking about their *internal* world. At the beginning of every well-constructed story, the main character should be flawed in some way; their "normal world" is broken. When you're developing a character for any type of

film, make sure that you give them a very clear flaw, and the more you know about this flaw the better. From where did this flaw come, what specific event caused it, etc.? As we will see later, clearly defining your character's normal world is an indispensable quality for story-driven films! But even in character-driven films, you'll find that characters with some sort of well-defined brokenness are immediately more fascinating; they are automatically more compelling and complex.

In future chapters, we will discuss the components that make up the "normal world" of your main character. It's important to note, however, that what you *do* with that normal world of your character will differ depending on the type of story you're telling. For example, the goal of the *story-driven* film is to take your character from an *old* normal to a *new* normal (from a broken normal to a healed normal), but the goal of the character-driven short film is not necessarily to take your character on any sort of a journey at all. Instead, the purpose of the character-driven short film is to simply watch a very interesting character live out their life for a set amount of time – no real beginning or end, just a chronology of events in the day-in-the-life of a character.

If your desire is to write characters that experience some sort of internal change at the end of the film – in other words, you want to move your character from point A to point B - then you need to read to the end of the chapter. If your character is going to experience any sort of internal change in your film at all, then you will need to incorporate elements of the story-driven film into your underlying structure.

Although *Some Folks Call It a Sling Blade* and *Peluca* are great examples of character-driven films, they are not *pure* character-driven films. Even these excellent examples rely on story-driven elements to make their narratives work. Although the pure character-driven film is a tempting format for the filmmaker, it (like the abstract film) can be very polarizing. When making character-driven films, you run the risk of boring your audience very quickly, which is why this format works so well in the realm of short films. If your desire is to create a *character-driven* film, then keep your film brief – just a few minutes in length.

It's important to keep in mind that audiences have been wired to hear stories since the beginning of time. As we will discuss in a moment, audiences try to find meaning in films, even if no meaning exists. Hollywood and audiences want stories, so even if you just want to explore a character on film and avoid telling some huge overarching narrative, you will still do yourself a favor if you weave basic story elements into the structure of your film. Audiences (and Hollywood) want structure!

**4. What is your character's worldview (how do they solve problems)?**

This is one of the single most important questions that you must answer about any character you create! Answering this question will add deep layers of complexities to your characters and, ultimately, to your stories. Both characters in the above case study have a very skewed and eccentric approach to how they engage the world. Their methods of confronting and dealing with problems are very different from "standard" ways of problem solving. In *Peluca*, Seth's answer to his friend's recent, self-induced baldness is to buy him a wig, but at the department store he finds himself in conflict. He only has enough money for one item and as he peruses the store, he discovers the "perfect" fanny pack on sale. In Seth's world, these things are of massive importance; they drive him. I don't know too many people who are "driven" by finding the perfect fanny pack or by helping a buddy cover up his nonexistent coiffure. If I did, then Seth's character might not be that interesting to me. Why would anyone care that deeply about wigs and fanny packs? I don't know, but I want to understand, and so... I keep watching.

In *Some Folks Call It a Sling Blade*, Karl's answer to his home-life problem is murder, but it's his childlike innocence juxtaposed against his morally debased actions that make Karl complex and riveting. How could anyone do the things Karl did? I'm not sure, but I want to understand, and so... I keep watching.

Had Karl been your typical, caricaturized Hollywood version of a murderer, he would not have been a compelling character to watch, even for just a few minutes. What made Karl interesting was the seeming mismatch of his external world with his internal world; in other words, he had a captivating worldview.

Pull from your own experiences and observations when creating your character. Who are the people in your life that you simply can't take your eyes off of - the quirky aunt or uncle with their crazy idiosyncrasies; the life-of-the-party who lives a gregarious, flamboyant lifestyle; or the wallflower who goes unnoticed but is reeling with emotional complexities? In writing the character-driven short film, you want the nuances of your film to come from the uniqueness of your main character, not from their quirky environments or from an interesting *concept*.

Though we will address the concept-drive short film in the next section, there are a few things regarding "concepts" that we need to address before we end our discussion on the character-driven film. If you start your character-writing process by saying, "I want to make a film with dinosaurs in it," or "I want to do a comedy," or "I want to make a film noir," you're not beginning with a character; you're starting with a concept. Concepts are fine, but a concept by itself is flat.

For example, a film-noir concept driven sounds great, but without well-developed characters, it runs the risk of being a really cool, black-and-white detective film that completely lacks substance. In a poorly constructed concept-driven film, the characters simply become props to help the filmmaker realize their ideas; the people in their stories are of no more importance than the gun in the detective's back pocket. This is not to say that concept-driven films can't have amazing characters. In fact, they should! But we will discuss how to develop characters for the concept-driven film later.

We are riveted by well-crafted, character-driven films because we want to learn as much as we can about the deeply fascinating characters we see unfolding before our eyes. For this reason, the character-driven story is very well suited for the short-film format. As we discussed in the chapter on abstract films, when audiences go to the movies, they are programmed to look for a story. An audience will engage a film that lacks typical story structure for a few minutes. A purely abstract film can hold the attention of your audience for a few minutes. Incorporating an interesting, well-developed character into your movie might buy you a few more minutes. But, if your story lacks structure and your character-driven film is any longer than ten minutes or so, your audience will become restless. Unexplainable programming embedded deep within your audience's brains will begin to long for a greater reason as to why they're watching your film. Their minds will search for structure and if no structure exists, they will lose interest and become irritated; you don't want to leave your audience frustrated.

So keep these two things in mind as you write your character-driven films. First, give your audience just enough of your interesting character and end the film before their brains kick in and begin to demand a deeper reason for watching your movie (about ten minutes or less). And secondly, if you want to engage your audience for a longer period of time, you will have to construct some sort of story (a character trying to solve a problem) into your film.

## CASE STUDY #1
*Some Folks Call It a Sling Blade* (1994)

Besides being a great example of a *character-driven* film, *Some Folks Call It a Sling Blade* uses several cinematic tropes that add to the intrigue of its subject matter and style.

The most notable trait in this film is the fact that, despite being a character-driven short film, it still has loose story elements that hold the film together. Karl is the character we find most compelling (and the character with whom we spend the most time); the film exists for the purpose of giving audiences a chance to delve into the world of this fascinating character. But the film has a running time of 25 minutes. So how was George Hickenlooper able to keep audiences interested in his character-driven film for that long? It's because he incorporated a subtle story into the background of his film. As fascinating as Karl Childers is, it's the character of reporter Teresa Tatum, played by Molly Ringwald, that drives the story. She is the one who faces the biggest narrative challenge in the film. Although Karl Childers will always be regarded as the main character in this film, from a structural perspective, Teresa Tatum is actually the film's protagonist.

The story begins on one of the most significant days in Karl's life – the day he's being released from prison. This is Teresa's one and only chance to interview Karl before he's released into mainstream society. Teresa HAS to get the story before it's too late; she has an external goal; she has a deadline and she has to overcome many obstacles to achieve her objective; in other words, Teresa Tatum is the character with the "story."

If you want to create a longer character-driven film, try incorporating elements of story into your structure, even if it's a secondary character with the goals and objectives.

In addition to incorporating story tropes into his film, Hickenlooper used a few other cinematic techniques to strengthen the experience for his audience. A good technique that every filmmaker can and should use is the technique of bookending their films. Open and close your film on images that are either similar or complement each other in some way. In the *story-driven film,* we see how important these opening and closing images are. In his book, *Save the Cat*, Blake Snyder stresses the importance of these moments. In fact, the "Opening Image" and the "Closing Image" are the first and last "beats" in Snyder's now famous 15 Beats of Scriptwriting; they show us what the world looks like *before* the story begins and what the world looks like *after* the story is complete.

Hickenlooper bookends his film by opening and closing the film in the same location (the "holding room"). This simple tactic gives the film a stronger sense of structure.

Lastly, Hickenlooper did a great job of establishing the rules of the universe: What's the one weapon a reporter has? It's their ability to ask poignant questions. But before the interview, Teresa is given one rule: "Don't ask questions!" This immediately adds tension to the story. Our main character is deprived of her most valuable asset; she must conduct an interview without asking questions. See what happens to your story if you handicap your main character – if you limit or take away from them their greatest strength.

And lastly, Hickenlooper didn't forget the visual medium in which he was working. He used the environment to his advantage. Karl doesn't like fluorescent lights, which immediately sets the stage for a visually interesting and compelling film.

## CASE STUDY #2
*Peluca* (2003)

Despite being quite different from *Some Folks Call It a Sling Blade*, *Peluca* follows many of the same story tropes. Jared Hess did a masterful job of creating the fascinating character of Seth, played by Jon Heder – a character that we'll watch do just about anything. Hess follows the rules of *character-driven* short films that we discussed earlier. Seth is an offbeat, interesting character with a unique worldview. Hess sets the film in a "day-in-the-life" of our main character and he bookends the story with the "bus" scene, which represents the beginning and end of a typical school day for Seth.

But despite being a *character-driven* short film, we once again see a few basic elements of story emerging. One great thing that "story" does for your film is it automatically begs your audience to ask the question, "What happens next?" The story element in *Peluca* is nonsensical and unimportant, but it gives the film a purpose; it gives the characters a stage upon which they can play out their quirkiness for audiences.

The reason *Peluca* exists (just like *Some Folks Call It a Sling Blade*) is for the soul purpose of exploring a main character. But character exploration works best when the main character has something to do – an objective – a story. In *Peluca*, Seth has something to do. Unlike Karl, Seth really is our protagonist. Seth is the character in the story who is on a mission; he wants to buy his friend Giel a wig.

The story starts on a significant day; it's the day after Giel decides to shave his head because his hair makes his head hot. Seth decides to buy Giel a wig, but once at the store, Seth must decide whether to help his friends or buy something he wants instead. These are all trivial scenarios, but they are physical, visual situations that give Seth cinematic opportunities to visually act out his worldview as opposed to stating it in dialogue.

As is the case with all types of stories, the character-drive film has its drawbacks. Without any story elements, audiences will engage fascinating characters for just a few minutes. If you want to make slice-of-life, character-driven films, you need to remain in the realm of short films. Film festivals are riddled with many character-driven feature films that explore interesting characters (with little to no story) for 90-plus minutes. These films can be interesting, especially if you can somehow relate to the character, but if your character-driven feature film truly lacks a story and we're left watching a character stumble through their lives without any objectives, you can rest assured that your film isn't going to get noticed by the masses.

Abstract films are a great place for filmmakers to learn, explore, and practice the *language of cinema*, and character-driven films give filmmakers a chance to wrestle with the intricacies of developing a fascinating *character*. And, the filmmakers who possess the ability to combine these two elements – *language of cinema* and *character* – will set themselves apart from other filmmakers.

## CONCEPT-DRIVEN SHORT FILMS

The next category of films we want to look at is the *concept-driven* story. We won't spend too much time discussing this type of film because this is the type that you and many other filmmakers have, more than likely, already attempted to make, and unfortunately, most concept-driven short films aren't really all that great. Festivals are overrun with concept-driven films and unless you know how to approach these types of films, more than likely you're going to write concept-driven stories that have lots of interesting visuals but absolutely no heart.

So what is a concept-driven film? A concept-driven film is one that exists for the purpose of exploring an idea (or a concept) as opposed to exploring a character or a story. Films like *Transformers*, *Jurassic Park* and *Twister* are all examples of concept-driven films. No one goes to see *Transformers* to watch the character of Sam Witwicky go on a compelling internal journey of personal transformation (pun intended). Instead, we go to watch *Transformers* to see cars turn into robots.

Sam Neil's character, Alan Grant, is an interesting character, but his character is not why we all rushed to theatres in 1993 to see *Jurassic Park*. We went to that particular movie to see a fascinating concept unfold – genetically engineered dinosaurs that reek havoc on a bunch of unsuspecting characters.

The allure of the concept-driven film is the fact that these types usually lend themselves very well to visuals – dinosaurs, robots, tornadoes. These are all things that the masses will pay big bucks to see, which is why the concept-driven film is one type that Hollywood loves.

Since this book is about parlaying your short filmmaking endeavors into feature filmmaking careers, we'd be remiss if we didn't at least address this important type of film. So, why then do we discourage students from making concept-driven short films? Our reservations have little to do with the final product (there are many great concept-driven films out there). We discourage students from making these types of films because of the process often associated with creating them. It all has to do with where you start, and with concept-driven films, most beginning filmmakers start there and never go any further. Starting with a cool concept is not a great place to begin. The best stories come from characters, not from concepts.

So, how then does one make a concept-driven film that's thought provoking, intelligent and compelling? You do so by backwards engineering your concept.

In the next chapter, we will talk about how to start with a character and find a story that best suits the character you've created. As we proposed earlier, when developing your characters, ask yourself this question, "What's the worst thing that could happen to my main character?" The answer to that question is one of the easiest ways to pull a story out of your main character. But, if you're starting with a concept, finding the story inside the concept can be more difficult. If you're beginning your writing process with a concept, work backwards and ask yourself this question, "Who is the one person in the world who would be the most deeply and personally impacted by this concept?"

*Jurassic Park* would not have been nearly as interesting had the main characters been run-of-the-mill civilians. Instead, all of the characters in the world of *Jurassic Park* had an intense interest in the world of science, wildlife and dinosaurs. In a sense, the people in *Jurassic Park* are people who should have known better. They were the people who should have been able to avoid the problem to begin with – they were the experts. The fact that the experts were incapable of avoiding the fate of dinosaurs running rampant inside an amusement park made the intensity of the situation even higher. Conversely *The Lost World* seemed to fall apart once the T-Rex made it to the mainland and began attacking everyday people like you and me; at that point, the film lost all sense of character and began to parody itself. Spielberg could have gotten away with it had that portion of the story happened earlier in the narrative; but unfortunately, he chose to focus on the concept of dinosaurs at a point in the story when the protagonists should have been our central focus.

Likewise, *Twister* is not a story about a bunch of everyday Midwesterners who hide in their basements every time a storm rolls into town. *Twister* is about the people who proactively seek out tornadoes.

Concept-driven films can be compelling if writers take the time to thoroughly develop the characters within the conceptual worlds. The movie, *Contact,* is a concept-driven film with a very well constructed, multi-layered protagonist played by Jodie Foster. Most people went to see *Contact* because it looked like a fascinating sci-fi film; we didn't go see the movie to watch a story about a woman who grapples with matters of faith and learns to come to terms with the death of her father, but those elements are all present in the movie and those are the elements that give *Contact* its heart.

It's very common for students to come to our workshop sessions and make blanket statements like, "I want to write a detective noir film," or "I want to make a teen comedy." But, when we ask those students to tell us about the main characters in their stories, we usually hear vapid responses like, "The main character is just some guy." Or they describe a very bland, everyday character that's both uncompelling and boring. What will make your concept-driven film fascinating is if your concept is happening to a very interesting person who is deeply and personally affected by your concept.

The show, *The X-Files,* was riveting because of who the main characters were. Fox Mulder was on a quest to prove the existence of aliens because he believed his sister was abducted when they were children; he desperately needed validation to prove he wasn't crazy and wanted to find hope that his sister still might be alive. Dana Scully was a person wrestling with her faith; she was the imperialistic doubter who needed tangible evidence in order to believe anything. *The X-Files* was fascinating, not because of the concepts of government conspiracies and the possible existence of aliens (there have been plenty of boring documentaries produced on that subject matter); instead, what made the show fascinating was the fact that this concept was happening to the right people.

Some genres lend themselves heavily to concept-driven stories. Pure horror films and detective movies are high-concept story formats that focus more on concept than they do story. We don't go see a Sherlock Holmes movie to learn about the personal life of the world's greatest detective; we go to watch him solve a mystery. If your film relies heavily on concept and lacks in the character department, it is imperative that you strongly incorporate elements of plot and story into your structure in order for your film to work. George Lucas once said that a special effect without a story is a very boring thing. The same can be said for concepts.

So what exactly are these elements of story? We've hinted at them for the past two chapters and now it's time to land our narrative plane on the runway of *story-driven* films and get our hands dirty. What makes a **story** and how does one tell it?

## STORY-DRIVEN STORIES

At the beginning of each of my story seminars before I begin my lecture, I ask all of the students to tell me what *they* think makes a good story. I instruct them to think outside the box – no answer is a wrong answer. Students throw out all sorts of wild ideas, but in the end, most of my students demonstrate that they already possess a fairly good sense of what makes a story. Their collective definition usually sounds something like this:

*A story is typically a linear narrative about a character who must go on some sort of journey. This character will have to face all kinds of conflict and obstacles along the way and in the end, whether the character fails or succeeds in their quest, they usually learn something about themselves that they didn't realize before the journey began.*

This is actually a pretty good definition of a type of story with which we're all very familiar. If you've read the work of Joseph Campbell or Chris Vogler, or if you've ever sat through any sort of story class, then you've heard a definition like this previously. In his book, *The Hero with a Thousand Faces*, Campbell calls this type of story *The Hero's Journey*. The Hero's Journey is a model of storytelling that has its roots in ancient mythology and has been used as a pattern for storytelling *ad nauseam* in Hollywood for decades. Campbell was, by all accounts, a philosopher who studied a wide array of topics, ranging from religion, to psychology, to sociology and mythology. Campbell proposed that all great myths are basically recapitulations of the same story structure – a story about one character going on a single journey. This form is what Campbell called the monomyth (one myth) or The Hero's Journey.

Decades later, Chris Vogler took Campbell's very lofty and "heady" theories and reformulated them into a practical, easy-to-understand model for writers to follow. In his book, *The Writer's Journey: Mythic Structure for Writers*, Vogler made the keys to understanding myth accessible to the working screenwriter. He helped screenwriters incorporate Campbell's theories into their modern Hollywood movies.

Many books about story structure have been written since, but most are just a re-examination of Campbell's monomyth or Aristotle's theory of mythos which he wrote about extensively in his treatise, *Poetics* – the earliest known writings on story theory. Mythos is a story theory that deals primarily with plot and how it relates to the main character.

Blake Snyder, John Truby, Robert McKee, Syd Fields, Linda Seger and Chris Huntley are just a few story theorists who have written phenomenal books and articles on story theory and story structure for film and television. Each of these authors takes a slightly different approach to tackling the problems of story, but at the same time, their ideas share many things in common. When students ask me which author they should read, I tell them to read all of them, and find the one that resonates with them the most. Story is not an exact science!

In the chapter entitled, "Story Beats for Short Films," we are going to look at the work of Blake Snyder, whose theories are currently very popular in Hollywood. In his book, *Save the Cat*, Snyder proposes that all stories can be broken down into what he calls The 15 Beats. But before we get too far down the story structure rabbit whole, there are a few things we need to address.

I have never once lectured on story structure and been able to avoid the student who bemoans the idea of being put into a creative box – the self-proclaimed artist who refuses to be shackled to any type of formula. As frustrating as these students might be, I must confess, I have a soft spot in my heart for them. Why? Because I used to be one of them. Every creative person loves the idea of free-flowing artistry; we long for our uninhibited inner selves to take over our canvases and for our art to happen naturally. We want to close our eyes, feel and let the brush take on a life of its own, and there are certain mediums in which that type of "free styling" produces profoundly gorgeous art. But, I have found that feeling one's way through writing a screenplay (even a short screenplay) rarely, if ever, produces good work.

There is such a huge difference between confusion and provocation. I have critiqued so many short films shot by filmmakers who were trained in the art of filmmaking; they've shot from the depths of their hearts; they've artfully executed the language of cinema in all of their compositions and sequences... yet, they still created films that were utter and complete messes. And the reason why? Despite all of their training and their high level of visual literacy, very few of them have taken the time to learn some of the most basic, simple tenants of storytelling.

Hollywood tells story-driven stories; their films may be high-concept, but in the end, Hollywood films adhere religiously to the principles of story and follow structure to the letter. So, the first thing you must accept and understand about the story-driven film is this: *At its core, the medium of story-driven film is, first and foremost, a medium of structure.* I cannot emphasize this enough.

If you want to make films that resonate with people, films that audiences will want to see over and over again, films that people will enthusiastically talk about for days, then you more than likely have a strong desire to make story-driven films. Whether you realize it or not you probably want to tell stories that have "*...a linear narrative about a character who must go on some sort of journey. This character will have to face all kinds of conflict and obstacles along the way, and in the end, whether the character fails or succeeds in their quest, they usually learn something about themselves that they didn't realize before the journey began.*"

Or, in other words, you want to tell stories about characters trying to solve problems.

One of the main objectives of this book is to help you not only understand the kind of story you're telling, but also to help you figure out the kind of story you're NOT telling. It has been my personal experience as a writer, that the more I limit myself, the more creative freedom I find, and the writing process tends to unfold with noticeably greater ease. Orson Welles once famously said, "The absence of limitations is the enemy of art." It's much easier to write your story if you have ten options on the table as opposed to a thousand. Fig-

ure out the kind of stories you want to tell… and quit trying
to tell all the others.

Our goal is not to force any filmmaker to make only
one type of film, but rather to encourage filmmakers to practice (and master) the basics. A screenwriter who dutifully
studies the principles of story-driven stories is equivalent to
a pianist who religiously practices their scales.

We began our discussion on story by talking about
the two major categories of films: 1) the abstract film and
2) the realism film. From there, we divided the realism film
into three subcategories, a) the character-driven film, b)
the concept-driven film, and c) the story-driven film. In the
next three chapters, we are going to go even deeper and talk
about three different types of story-driven films: i) The Fable,
ii) The Fairytale, and iii) The American Myth.

As we explore these three different types of story-driven films, pay close attention to which ones work best
for short films. If you are currently writing a story, see if you
can identify which of the three story-driven categories (fable,
fairytale or American myth) your story falls into; once you
can place your film, you can defeat the "enemy of art" by adhering to the rules of that particular story type. For example,
if you discover you're writing a fable, then you can relieve
yourself of the unnecessary burden of trying to incorporate
all of the qualities of fairy tales into your story; your writing
just became infinitely simpler!

Before we delve into these three story types, there is
just a bit more ground we need to cover. Let's look at the
last two questions from our list of the **Six Crucial Character
Questions** that we introduced at the beginning of this chapter. We've saved these two questions for this section because
they deal specifically with characters and their story journeys.

### 5. What is the ONE external goal your character is trying to accomplish?

The external goal of your main character is the single most important element of your entire story. Without it, your story will meander; you will get frustrated because you won't be able to figure out where to take your story; and in the end, you'll more than likely give up and abandon your story altogether. The main goal of your character serves as the backbone of your script. It's the thing that, not only drives the plot, it oftentimes IS the plot.

There are reasons why sports movies work so well, it's because the external goal of the main character is so clear and obvious. We know from the very beginning that a sports film is going to end with a championship game and somebody winning a trophy – a final battle and a victory that are very external and easy to see. And, for the writer, EVERY story, whether it's a murder mystery or a love story, should have just as clear an external goal.

Depending on the genre, this goal may or may not be extremely obvious to the audience, but it should always be clear to the writer. For example, dramas typically have very subtle external goals; in fact, in a drama the internal problem of the main character (which we will discuss next) is usually the thing that drives the story. In some cases, the internal problem can be so strong that audiences might not even be able to recall what the external goal actually was. In a detective story, however, the external goal is very specific – "to solve the case." In fact, in detective stories and horror stories, the external goals can be so strong that oftentimes they completely overshadow the internal problems of the main characters altogether.

In *Lord of the Rings*, the external goal of the main character is about as obvious as you can get. Frodo must take the One Ring of Power to Mordor to be destroyed in the fires of Mount Doom. That one goal drives the entire narrative of

*Lord of the Rings.* However, in a drama like *Ordinary People*, the external goal of Calvin, played by Donald Sutherland, is to find a sense of health and normalcy for his family after the tragic death of their son – a clear goal that has external consequences, but a goal that's difficult to measure and one that leans more towards the internal world of the main character.

As as you begin your writing, I strongly encourage you to practice by starting with very clear external goals. Ask yourself this question, "Is my character's external goal cinematic?" Or in other words, "Can I take a picture of the moment my character achieves the goal?"

If I'm writing a romance story and I decide that my main character's external goal is "to find true love," I'm going to discover very quickly that writing this story is going to be exceptionally difficult. There are two things wrong with this goal. The first problem is the fact that "to find true love" is a very internal goal. I can't take a picture of a person achieving this goal, because it doesn't take place in the external world. It's possible for a person to find true love on the inside and their closest friends never even know it happened. "Finding true love" is a great goal in the real world, but not if you're trying to write a story.

The second problem with this example is this; if I asked a roomful of people to describe "what finding true love looks like," every person in the room would have a dramatically different answer to the question, which means, my goal is not specific enough. When formulating your external goal, you have to be as detailed and specific as possible. Is your goal measurable? Can you take a picture of it? If you answer either one of these questions "No," then keep working; your goal is too internal or too broad. I could write a million different stories about a man trying to find true love; I wouldn't even know where to start; I could write a story about dating, marriage, sex, teen romance… the list goes on and on. So, let's heed the words of Orson Welles and intentionally limit ourselves in order to make the process easier.

So, how can we make this goal more specific and external? What if I showed you a picture of a man down on one knee, staring into the eyes of a beautiful girl, while holding a diamond ring in his hand? Would you need any words to understand what was happening in that picture? Of course not; this man is asking a girl to marry him. So instead of our goal being "to find true love" let's change it to "to propose to a girl."

So we've added some limitations to the goal, but it's still broad and could go in many directions. So now what? One of the best ways to measure the strength of a story is to ask yourself this question: "Why now?" Or in other words, why should your audience tune into the life of this character at this particular moment in their life? Why not next week, or a year from now? Why does your character need to pursue this goal today? If there is no good reason for your character to pursue their goal right now, then your goal isn't strong enough. Increase the strength of your goal by raising the stakes and making the goal urgent.

So what if we rewrote the goal of this romance story to read, "to propose to a girl before his thirtieth birthday." Notice that the goal has become more specific, more interesting, and it's even beginning to suggest a genre; this story is starting to feel like a comedy.

But let's make the goal even **more** specific. One of the easiest ways to define your goal is by subjecting your main character to a time crunch; give them a finite amount of time to achieve their goal. We call this writing device, "the ticking time bomb." It adds tension and gives us a definite moment when the audience will know for certain whether or not the character has achieved their goal. So what if we wrote a one-sentence pitch for this story and it read something like this:

*"This is a romantic comedy about a man who has to propose to a girl before his thirtieth birthday… which is only two weeks away!"*

This is infinitely more specific than a story about a man looking for true love. Instead of a million options, I've now limited myself to just a few. Make the external goal of your main character as specific, as measurable and as photographable as you possibly can, and you'll suddenly find that your story is much easier to write.

So let's shift gears and talk about question 6:

6. **"What is the ONE internal problem your character needs to solve?"**

This is a crucial question to answer when telling story-driven stories; however, you may find it difficult to delve into the internal world of your character within the limited amount of time afforded to you by the medium of short films. But, even if you aren't able to fully explore a character's internal world, you, as the writer, should know the answer to this question.

When developing features, I have my students answer **multiple** questions about the internal worlds of their main characters. A discussion on this topic alone could fill multiple books because it deals with the deep psychology of your main character. It addresses the flaw inside your character that needs to be fixed, how that flaw came about, why your character has never addressed their flaw and what needs to happen in order for the flaw to be healed. If you're telling a drama, all of these important qualities need to be addressed, but for the short filmmaker, answering the above question alone is sufficient enough to begin the writing process.

The internal problem of your main character is emotional or psychological in nature and is typically broader than your character's external goal. In the romantic comedy example that we discussed above, we saw that "to find true love" did not make a very strong external goal. However, "to find true love" actually works very well as an internal problem. Your main character's internal problem should always be connected to your main character's external goal.

Sometimes the goal and the problem work together; the solution to your character's internal problem helps them achieve their external goal. But, sometimes the goal and problem work against each other; the solution to your character's internal problem actually works against the achievement of their external goal. So, here's where you, as a writer, can start to have a little bit of fun.

In our romantic comedy above, what happens when we keep the external goal of our main character the same, but we switch around the internal problem? Let's take a look:

EXTERNAL GOAL:   *"a man must propose to a girl before his thirtieth birthday… which is only two weeks away!"*

INTERNAL PROBLEM:   "…to find true love"
"…to seek revenge"
"…to earn the respect of his father"
"…to prove his power over women"

Notice how the external goal never changed, but by tweaking the internal problem, we dramatically alter the story we are going to tell; we open up some interesting new possibilities. And, notice how much the different internal problems affect the genre. With the above list, we could easily write a romantic comedy, a thriller, a tragedy or a horror, depending on which of the internal problems we choose. So, by answering this question, we've focused our story once again and made our screenplay easier to write.

Next, you must determine whether the internal problem of your main character is **positive** or **negative**. For example, "to find true love" is a positive problem, it's a goal worthy of pursuit; but "to seek revenge" is a negative problem, a character flaw that needs to be overcome. Keep in mind that your character can fail in finding the solution to their internal problem; this is advanced writing, and I encourage beginning students to stay away from such stories, unless you're writing fables. Fables can (and often do) end negatively which we will discuss in the next chapter.

And finally, you, as the writer, must know the **solution** to your main character's internal problem before you ever write one word of your script. The solution to your character's problem will more than likely be the theme of your film. For example, if the internal problem of your main character is "to seek revenge," the solution to might be "to learn to forgive." If that's the case then "forgiveness" is the theme of your film. A good writer is able to skillfully hint at the theme of the film from the very beginning of the story, but your character can't discover the theme (solution) until the end.

Everything we've covered in this chapter will serve as the basis for the chapters that follow. Continue to review the material we've presented here; experiment with characters and their external goals; see what happens when you develop a character but change their age or give them a different internal problem. Just remember that the more deliberate you are in answering the above questions, the more clear and focused your stories will be.

# CHAPTER FOUR
# FABLE SHORT FILMS

If you have decided your story is best suited for the realm of realism, then you must decide if the story is best structured as a fable, a fairy tale or a myth. What are the differences? How do you go about making such a determination? In the following pages, we take a serious look at how one goes about structuring a fable, a fairy tale or a myth.

It is important to recognize that, while we will provide basic ground rules for these various types of short films, film structure is not an exact science. Few disciplines that require moving human emotions are. While we feel we provide enough characteristics of certain story types to label it, there are always arguments that other labels might fit better. Keep in mind that these structural elements are not meant so much as technical rubrics for determining what a preexisting story or short film is, as much as they are tools for creating blueprints of certain types of stories and short films.

## THE FABLE

For our purposes, it is important to begin by defining the term "fable." The word "fable" is used throughout the history of literature; we are redefining or perhaps giving greater definition to the label. Bruno Bettelheim, in his groundbreaking work, *The Uses of Enchantment,* suggested that a fable is a cautionary tale that arouses anxiety and prevents us from acting in ways that are described as being damaging to us. Traditionally, fables have often featured animals and inanimate objects that take on the characteristics of human beings as central characters. Samuel Johnson put it this way, "A fable seems to be, in its genuine state, a narrative in which beings irrational and sometimes inanimate, are for the purpose of moral instruction, feigned to act and speak with human interests and passions."

We are going to embrace these traditional definitions and add a few other qualities and characteristics that are common when one is structuring a cinematic fable. First, a fable is a film that poses a question and provides a simple black-and-white, moralistic answer to the question. Sometimes, this is executed as a film that simply poses a question, where the filmmakers then heavy handedly suggest an answer to the audience that viewers are supposed to derive for themselves. Many times, these films are constructed for the purpose of sparking a particular conversation where a central theme is purposefully driven by the filmmaker. Filmmakers should be wary of the fact that these films can easily fall into the realm of propaganda.

Second, a fable is a story that typically was handed down from generation to generation. These stories often involve "truths" which were passed down from parent to child. And while the child readily espouses this "truth," it is likely that they have not experienced it themselves. Filmmakers should, in turn, be cautious that they are not attempting to espouse a truth that they have only heard, rather than one they have experienced themselves, as this is usually more transparent to the audience than to the filmmaker.

Next, a fable features simple, flat characters. Complex characters are for the mythic structures that we will discuss later. Often filmmakers are taught to avoid flat characters. However, for the purpose of constructing a fable in the short film, flat characters are quite necessary. The main character typically represents laziness, greed, envy or some other basic human trait or emotion and the story revolves around what happens when they encounter a character who represents the opposite trait or emotion.

Much like Carl Jung suggested about our dreams, all characters in a fable represent a different side of ourselves. Fables are not meant to teach that the faithful worker always wins over the lazy worker, but rather that the faithful part of yourself is more skillful for us than the lazy side. In other words, despite common logic, fables are not meant to convey how we should act in relation to others, but how we should react to the lesser tendencies of our own nature.

In the traditional fable, *The Ant and the Grasshopper*, the ant is clearly the character we are meant to emulate. However, the ant is quite nasty to the grasshopper in the end and chooses to let the grasshopper suffer, feeling that he deserves it. The lesson here is not to look down on those who have not made the wise choices we have. Instead, it is meant to call forth the side of ourselves prone to hard work and, when we choose not to take this route, the outcome is deserved. We have no one but ourselves to blame. For these reasons, fables tend to be internal stories told with external metaphors.

In many ways, fables are quite formulaic. They are definitive, which can be both a strength and a weakness, as we will discuss later. Bettelheim suggested, "Often sanctimonious, sometimes amusing, the fable always explicitly states a moral truth, no hidden meaning, nothing is left to the imagination." These types of short films will appeal to a certain style of filmmaker. The personality of some storytellers doesn't desire to wrap their worldview inside the depths of character and plotlines. Some would rather offer an unmistakable clarity to how the world should be. Fables appeal greatly to this style of filmmaker. Audiences who prefer to see certain truths about the world in black-and-white terms will gravitate toward these types of stories as well.

## THE POWER OF A SIMPLE TRUTH

Young filmmakers often will associate the complexity of their story with the maturity of their storytelling. The old adage of "simple stories and complex characters" sometimes does not ring true for a storyteller until they have released a number of complex stories from their system. Indeed, some never are able to overcome the temptation. However, the most profound truths are usually the simplest ones. Simple stories are not the sign of a filmmaker without something to say, but instead are the mark of one who realizes that simple tales are the most universal. They are understood across cultures, age groups and personalities.

It is interesting that the simplest stories within a culture are often considered the domain of children. However, the simple lessons and truths of these stories are usually ones with which adults struggle throughout their lives. How many adults have truly managed to avoid the tendencies of greediness? How many have surpassed the struggle against laziness? Who never fails to have the right attitude when times are difficult? The simple truths found in fables can be the most powerful in all of storytelling when presented with a certain humility and respect for the audience.

Having said this, it should be noted that not ALL truths are simple. Some issues are truly best left in shades of gray. Not every story should be contained within the structure of a fable. Some stories require much more setup and backstory than a fable affords. Other stories are more about how we interact with other humans and the conflict that arises from these interactions. Keep in mind that, in its purist form, a fable is a very internal story told with external metaphors. Stories where a protagonist's clearest goal is external are better executed in one of the other forms (fairy tales, myths or American myths), as opposed to internal manifesting in a simple external task.

## STRUCTURE FOR FABLES

When structuring a short film fable, there are really two key sequences that should be in place – the problem sequence that presents two opposing characters or forces holding different philosophies for success and the solution sequence that presents us with the one character's or force's accomplishment of a certain moralistic victory. In addition, the solution sequence is best given to the audience in a way they do not anticipate, with some sense of dramatic irony.

Fables, however can be built with more developed structures and woven together with beats commonly found in other types of stories. A fable often has a catalyst and is told in the typical three acts. The first act sets up the world of the fable and usually ends with defining the two opposing characters. The second act sets up the action of the story, usually revolving around the two opposing characters performing the same, or similar, tasks. In many fables, the antagonistic character seems to be succeeding in the task more so than the protagonistic character. These first two acts may occur quite quickly. Together they comprise the problem sequence. The third act presents the solution sequence. It is in this sequence that we see the advantages the antagonistic character had seemingly crumble away. The character with the more socially accepted moral argument or quality always must be the victor in a fable.

In some fables, the victor's victory is subtle and, in some cases, non-existent. However, the character that suffers defeat never does so in a subtle way. The defeat is always quite clear and pronounced, even if there is no clear victor. In a good story, an antagonist should have a strong, but flawed, moral argument. The fable is the only story type in short-film structure where the antagonist can actually be the main character and often is. An example of this from literature is

Aesop's fable, "*The Town Mouse and the Country Mouse*." For those unfamiliar with the story, here is a brief summary:

A mouse that lives in a town goes to visit his cousin who lives in the country. The country mouse rolls out his finest vittles for the visiting cousin, including bacon and beans. The town mouse is appalled at the food his country cousin daily dines on. He insists on taking him immediately back to town where they can feast on the finest treats for which a mouse could ask. Upon arriving in the city, the mice head for the fanciest restaurant in town and begin feasting on the most luxurious scraps in the garbage – steak, breads and wine. However, during their dinner, a dog comes for his own meal from the trash. The mice both make a mad dash for their lives. The country mouse concludes that it is better to eat beans in peace than to eat steak in fear.

In the tale, it is presented as the town mouse's story. He is the central character, but is effectively the antagonist. It is the country mouse that learns a lesson. It is the country mouse that experiences the character arc. The story never gives an indication that the town mouse is any different when the story ends than when it began. In effect, the town mouse, our antagonist, is our main character. While this is not required to be an effective fable, as there are plenty of fables where the protagonist is the main character, it is not uncommon.

This structure might be effective for a person who has decided that they want to work within the realism, but do not wish to simply perform a character study and a deeply flawed, but interesting, antagonistic character. If a filmmaker wishes to work in a story-driven structure, but focus deeply on the antagonist in their story and perhaps present them as the main character, the fable might lend the most viable option.

## THE HORROR FILM FABLE

Fable structure is not widely used in the feature-film arena. Exceptions include stories where the filmmaker wants a very explicit moral ending, typical in many "Christian films" and, on the opposite end of the spectrum, "exploitation films." The one feature-film genre where fable structure often is used is that of horror. While many horror films are structurally horror myths, there remains a popular type of horror film that still uses fable structure. The horror short film fable is a grossly underused story type that lends itself to a manageable structure that can be tackled by filmmakers early in their development.

These types of horror films often feature a particular sin committed by townspeople, high school students or individuals for which there must be atonement. Like the Biblical tale of Sodom and Gomorrah, there is usually one character found worthy of salvation amongst the soon-to-be-punished others. This worthy soul usually serves as the protagonist of the story. However, they are rarely what make the story memorable.

The antagonist gets to shine in these stories. Their moral argument is strong in that the "sinners" in the story deserve punishment. However, the antagonist's ethical superiority is flawed because the punishment they dole out is far more severe than the crime committed, usually death. Examples of these antagonists in the feature-film arena are plentiful and include horror icons; such as, Jason Voorhees, Michael Meyers and Freddy Krueger. However, even classic horror films use similar elements. Certain versions of the Frankenstein and Dracula stories are fables as well, providing a very simple moral lesson about rejecting those who are different than we are.

Short-film horror fables are structurally sound templates to work in as long as they feature the two required

sequences – the problem sequence that presents two opposing forces holding different philosophies for success and the
solution sequence that presents us with the one force's accomplishment of a certain moralistic victory. They also must
dictate the required black-and-white parameters of morality,
along with the consequences of immorality.

Some modern flavors of horror toy with other structures of storytelling, particularly myth and the American
myth, as fairy tales do not seem to lend themselves as readily to horror. However, even those horror films that structure
themselves in a more complex manner often will take elements of the fable in order to more effectively tell their story.
It seems the thick lines that define morality in the horror
genre just naturally lend themselves to work within the fable's framework.

## WEAKNESSES OF THE FABLE

With the exception of the horror short film, fables
rarely demonstrate that you can move to the next level of
storytelling – fairy tales or mythic structure. Fables will
not help you advance your career if you desire to tell feature-length stories in Hollywood. Films that are as "mes-
sage-driven" and heavy handed as most fables tend to be,
usually cause Hollywood to bristle and assume that the filmmaker's message is more significant to them than their craft.

Fables can also suffer from the oversimplification of
complex issues, as well as the generalization of outcomes
that will not always be true. In his writing, Bettelheim reminds us of the fable, *The Little Engine That Could*. He suggests that because the fable is set in modern times when
trains exist, it leads us to believe the theme or truth can hold
in our modern lives and times without fantasy elaboration.
The theme that if you have the right attitude, you WILL
succeed is not always true, even though we would like to

believe it is. This can cause the story to hit a false beat in the heart of the audience or worse, make them feel as if the story is a lie.

If we create a fable that is set in our modern era or bares a great resemblance to our modern lives and attempt to make generalizations about truth and its place in our life, we must cautiously qualify our conclusions, which usually leads to bland storytelling. There is certainly a place for the short fable in the realm of storytelling. When these stories are ineffective, it is often because they are misused or the principles of a good fable are ignored. And while it might not demonstrate storytelling that is mature enough for the big screen, it can be excellent practice for the filmmaker who needs a short tale to hone their skills. It is also very useful to the filmmaker who is crafting a film to drive a particular conversation with their audience.

## USING ELEMENTS OF THE FABLE IN OTHER STORY TYPES

While telling outright fables in short films might not demonstrate a proficiency in storytelling that will move you toward the big screen, using elements found in fables just might. Fables will often contain character types, scenarios and subtle themes that are useful in telling the more complex types of stories we will explore in the coming chapters. Learning to take elements from fables that deeply resonate with audiences and utilize them in your story can have powerful results and extend the depth of the stories you are telling.

One of the most universal fables taught to children is the story, *The Boy Who Cried Wolf,* based on Aesop's fable, *The Shepherd Boy.* For anyone unfamiliar with the story, here is a brief summary:

A young shepherd is bored with his life and decides to cause some mischief by crying out that a wolf is eating the village's sheep. This causes a great deal of excitement in the village and some villagers even sit with the shepherd for a time and visit with him. The boy pulls the same stunt a few days later and the villagers respond again, but with a bit more frustration that there appears to be no wolf. A few days later, an actual wolf invades the village and eats up all the sheep. The boy's cries are ignored and go unanswered. A wise man tells the shepherd boy the following morning that a liar's words are never believed, even when he is telling the truth.

While this story has all the classics elements that make a good short-film fable, it is difficult to tell the story in a more complex format beyond this. However, there are elements of the fable that could easily be used in a fairy tale, a myth or even an American myth, all of which will be discussed in coming chapters. Many stories with more complex structure begin with a protagonist bored with their own life. In the fable, the protagonist creates his own excitement; he decides to do something to change this. In a more complex film, there would need to be a catalyst event to cause the character to make such a decision. The catalyst beat necessary for more complex stories, such as myths and American myths, is absent from a fable.

Another element easily taken from this fable and usable in many varieties of more complex stories is the theme of one man versus society. This, and perhaps other elements of this particular fable, are found in films such as Milos Foreman's, *One Flew Over the Cuckoos Nest*. Building on this idea of theme, the moral of the fable – that even when a liar tells the truth, no one will believe him – is certainly a universal theme that can be applied to even the most complex story structure. We see elements of this played out in films such as Tom Shadyac's, *Liar, Liar*.

Even though themes from this fable find their way into these more complex stories, the story itself is not meant to serve the theme. In other words, unlike the fable, the theme isn't the point of the story, or even the most relied-on theme in the film. It requires some degree of experience and craft to be able to maturely determine what elements from a fable will universally play in a more complex story. However, this can be part of the use of making short-film fables.

Developing one's craft through the repetition of practice is truly the only way to mature as a storyteller. Too many new filmmakers today are determined to take their first (or second or third) short film out to the festival circuit without developing their storytelling craft. Creating short films for the purpose of your own education and development is one of the strongest reasons to engage in the activity. Learning the subtleties and nuances of good storytelling, then how to execute them through practice, is the only path to success in this discipline.

### CASE STUDY #1
### *A Mouse's Tale* (2007)

In the French short film, *A Mouse's Tale*, we see all the classic elements of a short-film fable. We have a clear problem sequence – a mouse, about to be eaten by a lion, negotiates a more tasty meal for the feline. Our problem sequence is set up quickly. We know for whom we are rooting – the protagonist. We know what their external goal is - what they are trying to accomplish. We know against whom we are rooting – the antagonist. In addition to these key elements in our problem sequence, it is made clear that animals have taken on human characteristics (they talk) as is common in the short-film fable structure.

We also have the all-important solution sequence with a bit of dramatic irony. When the lion ties string to the mouse's tale, ensuring his inability to escape, the mouse uses the string to eventually harness the lion and facilitate his escape. Within the solution, we find two very clear moral themes. The first has to do with the greed of the lion. If the lion had simply eaten the first (or second) meal offered to him by the mouse, he would have had a full stomach and not be ensnared by the mouse. His greed for more attractive options eventually leads to his demise. If we remember that both the lion and the mouse are meant to represent opposing forces of our own nature, we see multiple moral lessons about which sides of our nature should be allowed what they desire. The second moral theme deals with the resourcefulness of the mouse. Often that which seems to restrain us can be used to free us, if we have eyes to see such a solution.

This film does not ask us to consider WHAT the lion inside us may be. It does not try to dissect what might be a mouse inside you, but a lion inside someone else. It rejects exploring the gray matters. Instead, it presents a clear moral message that the lion inside you will be undone by his own greed but the mouse inside you might see how to take those things that hold you back and use them to create freedom.

## CASE STUDY #2
### *The Black Hole* (2008)

In this British short film, we can clearly identify elements of the short-film fable. We have an inanimate object, a black circle or hole on a piece of paper that has taken on magical, even subtle, human qualities. In a sense, the black hole has become a "genie in a bottle" granting our protagonist a certain wish or magical power.

We have our required problem sequence – a worker who desperately needs to escape the mundane, life-sucking, technology-driven life he has at his job. Then we have the solution sequence – the new life given by the magic black hole. In the film, we see the protagonist use the magic gift four times. The first use – to retrieve his coffee cup – is actually a positive use, which helps him solve a legitimate problem. However, the remaining uses of the magic are all driven by greed. We see our protagonist use the magical gift to steal candy from a vending machine, to open his boss' locked office and finally to steal money from the company safe. The clear theme and moral message of the film is that greed will be your undoing. We could even assume a slightly more complex theme, that if we are greedy with the wonderful things we are given, it will destroy us in the end – a simple message many parents try to impart to their children.

The film doesn't ask us to consider how the protagonist might have used the magic to accomplish good for the world. Instead, it simply states that human beings will take the wonderful things they have control over and they will quickly use them for selfish and greedy purposes, which will lead to their demise.

# CHAPTER FIVE
# FAIRY TALES

*"When I was ten, I read fairy tales in secret and would have been ashamed if I had been found doing so. Now that I am fifty, I read them openly. When I became a man, I put away childish things, including the fear of childishness and the desire to be very grown up."*

- *C.S. Lewis, 1952*

## SETTING UP FAIRY TALES

This structure is perhaps the most recognizable to sto rytellers, at least in name. We grow up with the understanding that fairy tales are the domain of children and that they are usually read to children as entertainment before bedtime. Some of the more astute might even be aware of the lessons many fairy tales contain for children and that the stories can even contribute to a child's socialization and development. Albert Einstein suggested that if you wanted your child to be great, read them fairy tales, and if you wanted your child to be truly great, read them more fairy tales. But just what exactly is a fairy tale? Few of us could actually name a fairy tale that tells the story of a fairy. So what are these stories? What makes a story a fairy tale? How is one crafted and what types of stories lend themselves to being structured in the form of a fairy tale? We must remember that telling a fairy tale is about enriching one's experience. If the story turns into a cautionary tale, it becomes a fable.

While J.R.R. Tolkien preferred to often explain the role of myth in our lives, C.S. Lewis had much to say about fairy tales. Lewis was once quoted as saying, "The logic of a fairy tale is as strict as that of a realistic novel, though different." Bettelheim suggested one of the distinct marks of the fairy tale was that it was about the everyman, common people just like us. For this reason, the names in fairy tales are often generic and descriptive. Many characters don't even have names at all and are referred to as father, mother, stepmother or the poor woodcutter.

The set up for a fairy tale is quite distinct. In literature, they often begin, "Once upon a time," "In a certain country," or "A thousand years ago." These openings let us know that what follows does not pertain to the here and now in which we live. From here, the story usually proceeds in a realistic way: a mother tells her daughter to go and visit grandmother all by herself, a poor couple are having trouble feeding their children, or some other similar scenario. Sometimes, the opening of a fairy tale will begin to provide us with the rules for the world we are entering. A classic example is from *The Frog King*, which opens, "In older times when wishing still helped, there lived a king whose daughters were as beautiful…"

Short-film fairy tales should be set up the same way. It is important that the audience be given some basic rules for the world that they are entering immediately. Those rules might be as mundane as portraying that nothing exciting ever seems to happen in this world or is as exciting as the demonstration of magical elements appearing on every corner. The set up of a fairy tale should convey that these events happened "once upon a time, in a far and distant land" and make it clear that it offers food for hope, not necessarily realistic accounts of what the world is like.

The catalyst for a fairy tale is often the death of a parent or some other profound loss that the protagonist experiences. This loss will be the event that sends our hero on their journey.

## THE TRUTH IN FAIRY TALES

Bettelheim said, "Although these stories are unreal, they are not untrue: that while what these stories tell about doesn't not happen in fact, it must happen as inner experience and personal development." In other words, fairy tales get to the heart of an ideal – how the storyteller wishes the world would be. Bettelheim goes on to say, "While fairy tales invariably point the way to a better future, they concentrate on the process of change, rather than describing the exact details of the bliss eventually to be gained." In actuality, a fairy tale is a process that occurs within a protagonist. The label we assign to a story, be it fable, fairy tale or American myth, really speaks to the process that occurs inside the character over the course of the story and how that relates to the outside journey they make. In fairy tales, internal processes are turned into pictures. For example, when Cinderella experiences the death of her mother, we aren't told that she grieved or mourned or felt very lonely, but instead that every day she went out to her mother's grave and wept. Bettelheim concluded, "We don't describe a hero's psychological state in a fairy tale. Instead, we show him lost in a dense, impenetrable wood, not knowing which way to turn, despairing of finding the way out. To anyone who has heard fairy tales, the image and feeling of being lost in a deep, dark forest is unforgettable."

While literature might have more leeway to get away with just discussing this inner process our protagonist experiences, film is not nearly as forgiving. An audience will quickly be bored to tears having to watch a character go through an internal process, if there is no external metaphor of some sort to accompany it. In this arena, fairy tales in literature give us tropes to use as well. Often in fairy tales, our protagonist will find a magic object or acquire a magical power that changes the hero's life. This object or power will be the looking glass through which we see this inner journey occur. Most often, we see this played out in films through comedy. Feature films, ranging from Adam Sandler's *Click,* to Tom Shadyac's *Bruce Almighty* and *Liar, Liar*, provide fine examples of this. However, this structure is not limited to the domain of features. Short films such as *Control Z,* demonstrate the same structural set up.

While he might have preferred myths, Tolkien described that which is necessary in a good fairy tale. He included fantasy, recovery, escape and consolation – recovery from deep despair, escape from some great danger, but most of all, consolation. In order for these elements to be present, we must have a central conflict in a fairy tale. That conflict is usually embodied in an antagonist. In classic fairy tales, the antagonist was often a monster. According to Bettelheim, "Those who outlawed the traditional folk fairy tales decided that if there were monsters in a story told to children, these must be friendly monsters – but they missed the monster a child knows best and is most concerned with – the one he feels or fears himself to be." The presence of a strong antagonist, or monster, in a fairy tale can be one of the most significant (and relatable) elements in the story.

## WHY FAIRY TALES RESONATE WITH AUDIENCES

*"When one hears a fairy tale, (they) feel understood in their most tender longings, their most ardent wishes, their most severe anxieties and feelings of misery, as well as their highest hopes."*

*- Bruno Bettelheim, 1972*

Fairy tales often tell the story of the everyman. The protagonists in fairy tales are characters to whom we can relate. They are ordinary people, creatures or objects thrust into extraordinary circumstances. Bettelheim said that fairy tales tell stories about people very much like us. This characteristic is an important element in fairy tale short films as well. Protagonists in fairy tales we encounter in literature often are so common that they do not even have names. Instead they are generically referred to as Mother, Father or the woodcutter who lived in the woods.

Some psychologists who have studied fairy tales have concluded that the real question an audience faces when hearing (or viewing) a fairy tale is not if they want to be good or bad, but who they want to be like. It is certainly no coincidence that children for centuries have emulated a knight in shining armor or a damsel in distress. The truth is that many of us never outgrow these roles and we relate to characters who portray these qualities in the deepest part of our soul.

Bettelheim went as far as saying, "Fairy tales…more can be learned from them about the inner problems of human beings and the right solutions to their predicaments in any society than from any other type of story." If he was correct, then the inner problems of human beings have much more to do with whether we see ourselves as shining knights or evil ogres than if we have enough money to make us happy. Fairy tales, in many ways, are stories that help us deal with the issue of identity – who we really are. Dealing with this core universal question of, "Who am I?" makes the fairy tale an audience favorite. Good, short-film fairy tales will speak to this issue of identity in a way in which the audience can see themselves. Fairy tales are like mirrors; we should see ourselves in them.

Fairy tales should attempt to address other universal questions when possible: What is the world really like? How am I to live my life in it? How can I truly be myself? We will later learn that the answers given by myths are certain, while the fairy tale is more suggestive; its conclusion may imply solutions, but never completely spells them out. Audiences appreciate this about fairy tales because, in many ways, we are afforded the luxury of drawing our own conclusions. Fairy tales become fables when this option is taken from the audience. "One should never explain fairy tales, as they are meant to describe the inner states of the mind by means of image and actions," Bettelheim said.

Fairy tales, more than any other type of story, assure us in an area many of us fear most and develop the earliest fears of being alone or deserted. Our greatest satisfaction in a story's conclusion is that we will never be deserted. We love this device in story. Many boys will never forget the moment they first saw Han Solo come back for Luke at the end of *Star Wars*. The idea that someone will swoop in and rescue us from our loneliest moment is a concept that melts even the most jaded emotions. Perhaps this is why so many audiences cling to the most common fairy-tale ending, "And THEY lived happily ever after," never to be left alone or deserted. In this conclusion, we are reassured and given hope that, in the end, things really do work out.

## STRUCTURE FOR THE SHORT FILM FAIRY TALE

The structure we suggest for short-film fairy tales combines Tolkien's idea about the necessary elements for a fairy tale with Joseph Campbell's and Blake Snyder's takes on the hero's journey within a three-act structure, adding elements of what C.S. Lewis thought significant in a fairy tale. Tolkien said a good fairy tale consisted of escape, recovery, fantasy, and consolation. If we begin to place these elements into what we know about the journey all heroes (protagonists) must take, then we might reorder Tolkien's ideas to read fantasy, escape, recovery, and consolation.

Similar to the structure found in other types of stories, it's important in a fairy-tale short film that we establish the "normal" world and the "rules" of that world. This especially becomes important in a fairy-tale film because the "rules" and "normal" likely may look different than our world, though it doesn't have to. However, even if the world looks like ours, it will become necessary to incorporate an element of fantasy at some point. This could include seeing or hearing the life about which the protagonist fantasizes.

While Tolkien specifically said the element of escape in fairy tales was about escaping some great danger, we would add the idea of escaping the situations of the protagonist's "normal" world also is often an element. Because this is so common in fairy tales, we suggest that this decision on the part of the protagonist is a necessity in a short-film fairy tale. This moment is common in many structures. Blake Snyder called it the "break into two" or the moment that propels us into the second act of a story.

The second act of a fairy-tale film is usually all about the escape from great danger. The recovery of the protagonist is sometimes a restoration, but we would suggest that recovery is more about the decision the protagonist makes at the end of the second act which propels us into the third, or what Snyder referred to as the "break into three." The recovery sequence in the story also might consist of a series of challenges and recoveries that the protagonist encounters throughout the second act of the story. The end of the recovery usually happens when the protagonist decides to face the biggest challenge in the story, which will transpire in the third act.

Finally, Tolkien said that a good fairy tale held the element of consolation. This consolation is encompassed in the story's third act. While certainly the hero is consoled at the conclusion of their quest, this consolation also should be present in the audience. Short-film fairy tales almost invariably have happy endings. Even if the protagonist fails to accomplish their goal, the tone consoles the audience at the end. This often is seen in what Snyder referred to as the "final image." It gives us a picture of what life now will be like for our protagonist. The protagonist's new life is a picture of how the storyteller feels the world should be. This message will be suggested or implied, but never spelled outright. The inner journey of the character is given a visual image.

The consolation at the end of the story works most effectively when it has some sense of dramatic irony. As a matter of review for some, fairy tales (and myths) usually have one of four types of endings. A positive ending occurs when our protagonist gets what they want, as well as what they need, in the story. Positive irony occurs when our protagonist doesn't get what they want, but does get what they need in the story. A negative ending is when a protagonist gets neither what they want nor what they need in the story. Finally, negative irony occurs when the protagonist gets what they want, but not what they need in the story.

## COMMON TROPES & CHARACTERS IN THE FAIRY TALE SHORT FILM

*"I left the fairy tales lying on the floor of the nursery, and I have not found any books so sensible since."* — G.K. Chesterton

While structure is important in the fairy-tale short film, the symbolism, tropes, and use of certain types of character is equally, if not, more important. These tropes draw on universal concepts that cause audiences to resonate deeply with the simply story communicated in a fairy tale.

## PRINCES AND PRINCESSES IN FAIRY TALES

In many instances, fairy tales deal not so much with if we want to be good or bad, but who we want to be like. It's certainly no wonder that boys hear fairy tales and envision themselves as princes, while girls often take on the persona of the princess on the playground. While myths give us complex versions of humanity – people who are sometimes good and sometimes bad – fairy tales usually portray people as less nuanced. Characters will often be ideals of the way we would like to see ourselves.

## MOTHERS AND FATHERS IN FAIRY TALES

Parents are often an important part of fairy tales. They can represent a variety of things. First, they often act as a metaphor for our relationship to authority. In fairy tales, even when parents are wicked, we often see children remain loyal and subservient. Throughout history, this has served as a respectable method of dealing with authority. Most are aware, however, that oftentimes the children in fairy tales run away from the authority figures in the story, giving us another method for dealing with the issue. Rarely, if ever, do we see children seeking the death of a parent in a fairy tale. This sort of complexity would be better explored in a myth. We occasionally do see children seek out the death of evil authority figures, often in the form of wicked witches. It's also worth mentioning that parents in fairy-tale stories often do represent themselves. A mother in a fairy tale is often meant as a surrogate for our own mother.

## THE UGLY DUCKLING

Hans Christian Andersen first told the story *The Ugly Duckling* in one of his fairy tales. The trope became highly popular and often was used as the basis for a number of stories that featured unlikely heroes. Variations of the story include the "fish-out-of-water" story. Modern examples of this trope appear in stories ranging from *Being There* to *Forrest Gump* to *The Waterboy*. Blake Snyder suggested that these stories comprised an entire genre of films that he referred to as "Fool Triumphant" stories.

## MAGICAL BALLS IN FAIRY TALES

One of the most efficient ways that entire towns, cultures and societies are explored in captured time and space in fairy tales are through the use of parties, dances and royal or magical balls. This device gives the storyteller an excuse to gather everyone in the story to a central location at a certain time. This is especially helpful if there is a secret to reveal or a revelation to uncover. We then are able to see the reaction of everyone in the story at once. This device also serves as a ticking time clock in a fairy tale, in that usually a protagonist's external goal must be accomplished before this event. We often see this trope played out in modern fairy tales that take place in high schools, in the form of the prom or end-of-the-year dance. Again, here we are able to gather every subculture in the school together for a final unveiling of the protagonist.

## SECRET DOORS AND PASSAGEWAYS IN FAIRY TALES

The entering and exiting of new worlds has become part of the excitement in a fairy-tale story. Be it a looking glass, a wardrobe, or a Kansas cyclone, the "door" or passageway to a new place has become a significant element of the journey in fairy tales. One of the key characteristics of these secret doors is that they must be an unnoticed part of the protagonist's normal world. They are often common-place for the protagonist – something they see often, not realizing the wonder that lies nearby. It's also worth noting that the entry point into the new world is rarely the exit point – think Dorothy in *The Wizard of Oz*. While these doors can, and often are, literal, they can be metaphoric as well. Whether literal or metaphoric, the protagonist is often reluctant to go through the passageway. It often requires the encouragement of a "gate guardian" or other character before our hero can go through. This encourager often will join the protagonist for the journey that lies ahead.

## CONCLUSION

In all honesty, some of what is magical about fairy tales is a mystery within us. In his book, *C.S. Lewis On Story*, Lewis says, "It would be much truer to say that fairy land arouses a longing for he knows not what. It stirs and troubles him (to his life-long enrichment) with the dim sense of something beyond his reach and, far from dulling or emptying the actual world... He does not despise real woods because... with enchanted woods, the reading makes all real woods a little enchanted."

Some have been reluctant to construct modern fairy tales, fearing they might limit their audience to children. In truth, we never outgrow the power of fairy tales. We actually never stop telling fairy tales to each other. Instead, we change what we call them. The truths and tropes of these types of stories are just as powerful today as they ever have been. We would be wise to look at the way fairy tales use short-form storytelling powerfully and continue to find ways to incorporate this into our short-form filmmaking.

## CASE STUDY #1
### *Monster and Dumpling* (2011)

In this Asian, short-film fairy tale, we are immediately transported to a world where monsters and humans interact. We are quickly given the rules to this world. Our monster emerges as the protagonist who will experience the greatest change in the story. He has a clear external need: hunger, as well as a clear internal need: acceptance. His external need is met in a humorous and entertaining fashion. His internal need is met in a touching, dare we say human, way – he gains an unexpected friend.

Our clever storyteller also gives us a bit of dramatic irony when the character gets both what he wants AND what he needs. Our theme is universal in the story: If you give love a chance and are willing to sacrifice, it will pay off in the end. At the story's conclusion, that's exactly what happens – everyone lives happily ever after.

## CASE STUDY #2
### *The Fan and the Flower* (2005)

In this American short film, a lonely ceiling fan pursues his true love – a potted flower. Despite this story centering around inanimate objects, the characters and story are very fairy tale-esque. We have a protagonist who struggles with an inner need of loneliness. We have an external desire for the protagonist to be physically closer to the flower. We also have a theme of self-sacrifice, where the fan gives up both what he wants and what he needs for the sake of his true love.

The fan is thrust from his ordinary world of loneliness into a world where the possibility of love exists when the old woman who owns the house he lives in brings a flower to live in his room. We see the fan's many efforts to woo the flower. In this, we see ourselves. We see our own efforts to woo the ones we love. We are shown the rules of the world very early on. We can see that this fan is bound by the law that binds all ceiling fans. They must stay on the ceiling away from life and all they might desire. The conflict is the space that separates our protagonist from his true love.

We have a universal question about the nature of true love and what it requires. Our storyteller suggests to us that self-sacrifice is the path to true love. Finally, we have victory over loneliness. Despite the fan's self-sacrifice, he lives on in the heart of the flower. Though it is a bit more abstract, THEY live on happily ever after.

## COMMON CHARACTERISTICS OF THE FAIRY TALE SHORT FILM

- Short-film fairy tales tell the stories of ordinary men thrust into extraordinary circumstances. They serve as mirrors through which we should see ourselves.
- Short-film fairy tales should open by letting us know the rules of the world we are entering, as well as the relationship to the time, place, and reality in which we currently live.
- Short-film fairy tales usually begin by giving some background of a stressed relationship in the protagonist's life – usually familial. This could be the physical loss of a parent or child. It also could be the relational loss of a lover or spouse.
- Short-film fairy-tales' themes revolve around the heart of an ideal. They speak to how the storyteller feels the world should be.
- Short-film fairy tales should point the way to a better future for the protagonist, but focus more

specifically on the process of change.

- Short-film fairy-tales conflict is usually embodied in a single antagonist.
- Short-film fairy tales usually address a universal question. The audience then is allowed to draw out a conclusion from the story, lest the answer simply be offered and become a fable.
- Short-film fairy tales must have a happy ending that reinforces victory over one of the most common human fears – that we will not be left alone. It is important that THEY live happily ever after, not just the protagonist.

# CHAPTER SIX
# THE AMERICAN MYTH

*"Regardless of who you are and what you do, you can still be successful in America, fulfill your dreams and live within a fairy tale world."*

- Raymond Jones (regarding *Pretty Woman*)

The medium of feature films in American culture has necessitated a unique type of story structure, a formula that relies heavily on mythic structure, but ends like a fairy tale. "The American myth" is an updated form of ancient storytelling that values Western ideals over the antiquated values of past cultures. The difference between true myth and the American myth is evident by comparing their foundational theme; *American myth works to substantiate the hero's ego, whereas true myth seeks to destroy it.*

## ANCIENT MYTH AND THE WEST

Before we discuss the unique story structure of the American myth, let's delve a bit deeper into the history and origins of true myth. Hopefully, we'll be able to take off our modern lenses and view these stories with fresh eyes.

For the premodern audiences of classic myths, their stories were far more than entertainment. In fact, these tales ensured that their most valued traditions were passed onto future generations. Mythic stories preserved cultures, religions, values, and ways of life.

Many of these cultures that employed the use of myth had no connection with each other, but their stories all bore striking similarities. All ancient myths have heroes, mentors, epic journeys, specific missions, moral tests and antagonists. There are many facets of myth we'll discuss in this chapter, but there is one element strikingly absent from nearly every premodern myth. In order to continue our discussion regarding the genesis of myth, we need to "call out" this omission and recognize how its absence has affected our understanding of story. *With rare exception, most ancient myths lack the inclusion of female heroines.*

In ancient times, the guardians of culture – the ones writing the stories – were more often than not the male members of society. Western society has made positive strides in our fight for equal treatment of everyone despite a person's race, religion, gender, sexual orientation, etc. But, this wasn't always the case; women have spent millennia under the forceful oppression of men and the world has subsequently missed out on thousands of years of female storytellers. Most female protagonists have been confined to fairy tales. We rarely see them in myths. So to understand mythological structure, its origins and purposes, we have to recognize that nearly all of these stories came from the minds of men.

Mythological structure is a very male-driven structure. Although aspects of the structure resonate across genders, the process of the hero's journey is fundamentally a roadmap of the male psyche. The hero's journey serves as a model of problem solving for the masculine protagonist, his society and the male audience. It's a journey that culminates in an epic battle where the hero defeats a great evil and delivers to the world a metaphoric (or literal) elixir that remedies the maladies of society. But, before he defeats the villain and delivers the elixir to his community, he first must endure the mythic journey of the second act, the portion of the story that serves as a rite of passage for the hero.

Rites of passage, according to Richard Rohr in his book *Adam's Return*, are ultimate tests that culminate in a "journey from the false self to the True Self." Rohr concludes that the essential goal of the rite of passage is for the male initiate to learn that "life is hard; you are not that important; your life is not about you; you are not in control; and you are going to die."

It's a rather disparaging message for most Western moviegoers, but a thread has been woven into the fabric of nearly every ancient story since the beginning of time. The greatest lesson that the ancient young man could learn is that he is nothing – that his greatest purpose is to live and die for his community. For most of human history, life was not about self-actualization or the pursuit of passions, but about contributing to society and the greater good. But in modern, Western civilization, we have grown accustomed to philosophies, lifestyles and luxuries that make our interdependence on each other a low priority. The value of living exclusively for the good of one's society is practically non-existent.

Relatively speaking, Western civilization's egocentric system of thought is new; "modern thinking" had little influence on most of the classic tales from which we find inspiration. Some of our most cherished, ancient stories were written by people who lived during times when pursuing one's own desires was an abstract concept and, in some societies, even considered immoral. In fact, literary characters that chose to follow their own pursuits usually served as the villains in stories. Rohr says that a man who does not experience an initiation – or in our terms, a man who does not complete the mythic journey of the hero – will "always seek false power and likely will spend much of his life seeking prestige, perks and possessions," a description that could describe the value system of many Westerners… as well as the value systems of antagonists in many stories.

It would be easy to read stories like the *Epic of Gilgamesh* or *Argonautica* through a modern lens and miss the original themes of these tales altogether. If we adapted these stories for modern audiences, the temptation would be to tell an incomplete tale. We might choose to stop the narrative abruptly at the point when the hero succeeds in their quest, or we might place the emphasis on the hero's ascension to self-actualization, instead of placing a higher value on his "death to self." In other words, the emphasis would not be on the journey, but on the individual (the hero) instead – a very American ideal.

So, from where did this new type of storytelling originate? We have Greek philosophers, like Socrates and Plato, to thank for that. But, it wasn't until nearly twelve hundred years later that British philosopher John Locke postulated philosophies of individualism, freedom of religion and the rights of citizens that dramatically influenced the new Western world.

American Puritan colonial governor John Winthrop so strongly held to these philosophies that he suggested to a ship full of colonists that the world would be watching them to see if these "new ideas" worked and if these ideas were, in fact, of God. Winthrop warned of the inherent dangers of such a great calling. In his historic essay, *A Model of Christian Charity* (an essay imbued with fledgling ideas that many historians cite as instrumental in the development of the concept of the "American Dream"), written aboard the Arrabella while en route to 1630's New England, Winthrop cautioned the future colonists with these words: "For we must consider that we shall be a 'city upon a hill,' the eyes of all people are upon us; so that if we shall deal with our God in this work we have undertaken and so cause him to withdraw his present help from us, we shall be made a story and a by-word through the world." From the very beginning, the U.S. founding fathers intertwined individualism with their Christian faith – everyone is watching us, so we must do well in this new land. And, if our God is the one true God, He will help us realize our dreams. This hybrid philosophy would eventually morph into what we now call *The American Dream*.

According to Robert N. Bellah in his book, *The Good Society*, America has a long-held allegiance to individualism -- the belief that "the good society" is one in which individuals are left free to pursue their private satisfactions independently of others, a pattern of thinking that emphasizes individual achievement and self-fulfillment.

Western culture unashamedly values internal fulfillment above all else. Westerners resonate strongly with stories about heroes who overcome their inner demons and become stronger, self-actualized people. In our modern vernacular, we even have a saying for it: "Be the best version of you." Or in other words, *realize yourself!*

And, with just a slight theological spin, the Western Christian church proclaims the same message: "Life isn't about finding yourself; it's about discovering who God created you to be." In the movie, *Chariots of Fire*, Eric Liddell says, "I believe God made me for a purpose, but he also made me fast. And when I run I feel His pleasure." Western Christianity teaches us that we bring our Creator joy when we realize the full version of who He intended for us to be.

Christianity influenced Western though, and, in turn, Western thought influenced Christianity. Ultimately, we are a generation of people whose Christian theology and humanistic philosophies merged. We place the highest emphasis on being completely realized individuals and we put God's stamp of approval on that pursuit. It's no longer about the community; it's all about us.

And those are the stories we tell.

## CLASSIC MYTH AND THE FOURTH ACT

In true myth, at the end of the journey (after the world has been made better) our hero is left to contend with his own mortality. The severity of this contention varies from myth to myth, but it serves as a reminder to audiences that the journey was not for the benefit of the hero, but for blessing every man woman and child. This **anti-**Hollywood ending of classic myth serves as a warning to every listener who longs to be a hero; there is a dark side to even the most noble of callings. Even the purest of hearts cannot withstand the seductive power of the call. This portion of the story was so important to ancient cultures that, in some instances, it even required its own additional fourth act. To see this more evidently, let's take a look at the endings of four famous myths: *The Epic of Gilgamesh, Beowulf, Jason and the Argonauts,* and *Lord of the Rings*.

## THE EPIC OF GILGAMESH

*The Epic of Gilgamesh* is the oldest-known, written story, recorded sometime around 2,000 BC. The man, Gilgamesh, is considered by many historians to be an actual Sumerian king who lived around 2,500 BC. However, authors of the epic poem elevated Gilgamesh, the historic man, to god-like status, which was a common practice in ancient historical folklore.

The story of Gilgamesh is grandiose in scope. But at its heart, it's a simple tale about a man struggling with his own mortality. A major moment in the story is when Gilgamesh's companion Enkidu is killed in battle. Since Gilgamesh is part god, he is unable to comprehend death. Now motivated by the newfound fear of his own impending death, Gilgamesh sets out on a quest to uncover the secrets of immortality.

The bulk of the story adheres to many common storytelling tropes used in Hollywood films today. However, in the end, the story takes an unexpected twist and surprises modern audiences. Gilgamesh fails in his quest. There is no positive ending to this story. Although Gilgamesh may have learned a lesson in the end, the lesson humbles him; it diminishes him. One could argue that, instead of overcoming his flaw, Gilgamesh learns that he must live with it.

In the end, Gilgamesh does not become a better man by modern standards; instead, he learns that despite his supernatural lineage, he's just a man who is going to die.

## BEOWULF

In the story of *Beowulf*, Beowulf of the Geats comes to the aid of King Hrothgar of the Danes whose town is plagued by the monster Grendel. After several epic battles, Beowulf defeats Grendel and his mother. Beowulf receives fame and fortune for his triumphs as well as a stern warning from Hrothgar to avoid being boastful and to always honor the gods. Beowulf returns home and becomes king of his people. At the end of his reign, a fierce dragon descends on his town. Beowulf rises once again to fight, but this time he is mortally wounded. He dies an agonizing death and the story ends with Beowulf's tragic funeral.

In the story, Beowulf revels in the plunders of his exploits and his community is made better, but in the end, the authors felt it necessary to remind us that, despite Beowulf's bravery, he remained boastful and ultimately, had to face death.

## JASON AND THE ARGONAUTS

*Jason and the Argonauts* is a tale upon which many story structure theories have been based. All of the elements of great storytelling are present in this epic adventure. Jason is the quintessential epic warrior who sets off on a journey to the ends of the known world to find the rumored, magical Golden Fleece. Most film versions of this story end with Jason finding the fleece and returning to his kingdom. However, the full story of Jason's life ends tragically. Jason marries Medea, the daughter of the sun god, Helios. The townspeople soon become afraid of Jason's goddess wife and send them off into exile. In the end, Medea murders their three sons out of bitterness and revenge. Shortly thereafter, Jason dies when the stern of his rotting ship, the Argo, falls on him and kills him instantly – the same ship Jason used in his adventure to find the Golden Fleece.

Despite his cunning and prowess, Jason was manipulative, untrustworthy, and arrogant. He had vowed to love Medea forever and, when his heart wandered, she murdered their children. In the end, it was Jason's ship, the vessel that represented his mightiest accomplishment, that fell upon Jason and sent him to his grave.

## THE LORD OF THE RINGS

Thanks to Peter Jackson, the already-famous Tolkien myth, *Lord of the Rings,* has become a pop-culture mainstay. And with some notable exceptions, most critics agree that Jackson did a fairly good job of honoring the themes of the original text.

But in this epic story of good versus evil, even our amiable protagonist, Frodo Baggins, finds himself seduced by the One Ring of Power – the very thing he was sent out to destroy. While the thunders of Mount Doom roar, Frodo turns to Samwise and says, "But I do not choose now to do what I came to do. I will not do this deed. The Ring is mine." Even this lovable hobbit was incapable of making the right choice; his ego won in the end. But fortunately, through a random act of chance, in the end, good ultimately wins.

Upon destroying The Ring and returning to The Shire (which was decimated by fire in the novel), Frodo discovers that his life will never be the same. He cannot simply pick up life where he left it, so Frodo boards a ship destined for The West (Tolkien's version of the good afterlife). Tolkien was clear to note that once a person ventured to The West, they would "pass out of time and history, never to return" – an eternal separation from community - a metaphoric death. Frodo paid for his adventure with his life.

Each one of these epic stories ends with what could arguably be a prolonged third act, or an entirely separate fourth act. Ancient myths were not satisfied with simply sending characters on journeys and seeing the outcome. It was very important to ancient storytellers to write about the life of the hero *after* their journey was over. Often upon the hero's return, their mortality is made evident. It is usually at this point in the story that the "gods" abandon the hero; or the hero betrays the lessons learned; or the protagonist makes a tragic, moral compromise. Nearly all mythic heroes crumble under the weight of their own mortality and dissolve into obscurity.

As glamorous and magnificent as the mythic journey of the hero may seem, the calling is, in actuality, the most burdensome yoke one could bare and it ultimately demands the hero's life. Mythic stories were journeys in which the death of the hero ultimately mattered very little. The myth journey is never about the ego; in fact, in the four examples above, it was the egos of the heroes that ultimately proved to be their undoing. Ancient writers knew that, of all the demons that torture humankind, a *man's ego* is the most relentless. American myth exalts the ego; whereas, true myth fights against it. True myth is about the new, better world continuing on without the hero, in some cases, completely forgotten. It is rare in myth that the hero experiences the fairy-tale ending of "happily ever after."

Even the mythic character of Jesus Christ had to contend with his mortality at the end of his journey – and not by means of the death for which He is most noted. After Christ's crucifixion on the cross, he rose from the dead. But, Jesus' journey had so radically changed him and his community that he could not simply continue His physical life on Earth. So, He had to face his mortality once more and ascend to heaven, leaving us mere humans here to wrestle with, argue against, debate, and even slaughter those who oppose the elixir he brought to us – the message of eternal atonement for our sins.

However, the point in the Gospel narrative when Christ ascends into heaven is the place where most mythic stories end. But, when we take the entire canon of the New Testament into consideration, we discover that the Christian narrative does not end there. Ultimately, Christ's followers will be joined with Him in paradise for all eternity, or in other words, they (and Christ) will all live happily ever after. American stories have been heavily influenced by this deeply rooted Christian philosophy; no matter what happens to us in this life, in the end, everything will be okay.

Tolkien coined a term in his essay, *On Fairy Stories,* called the *eucatastrophe.* In story, the eucatastrophe is a sudden turn of events that saves the protagonist from experiencing a tragic ending. This concept has its origins in the Gospel myth of the Bible. The introduction of the character of Jesus Christ into the human narrative is the ultimate eucatastrophe; it's the event that ultimately leads to the supernatural redemption of all mankind.

The eucatastrophic character of Jesus Christ had a surprising effect on American culture and the stories we tell.

The universal hero of Christ inadvertently relieved many future generations of the burden of having to endure historic initiations into adulthood. The need to die for one's community began to lose its relevance, since the universal hero of Christ already had done so once and for all.

We no longer needed legends and myths. Slowly over time, we lost our need for heroes as the Christian tradition unintentionally destroyed the King Arthurs of future generations. The closest things we have to heroes in modern culture are *superheroes*. But even superheroes reflect the Christian belief in (and our desire for) a supernatural savior who comes from another world to save us all.

In contrast, the heroes of classic myths, whether of supernatural origins or not, were reflections of the common man. This hero may have relied heavily on help from the gods (or in the case of Gilgamesh may have even been part god), but it was ultimately up to the hero to battle and defeat his own ego-driven humanity in order to make his world a better place. And this is where the American mythic story diverges.

## THE AMERICAN MYTH AND THE MOVIES

Most American screenwriters take their hero on a three-act, mythologically inspired journey that rarely ends with the hero coming to terms with their own mortality. Instead, American movies typically end with the hero becoming a better person and everything in their world being made right. In fact, Hollywood is so known for these types of uplifting endings that when we hear someone say, "that movie has a Hollywood ending," we know what they mean. It means that the main character got what they wanted and what they needed. As we will see in the next chapter, all stories have two endings: the resolution of the protagonist's external journey and the resolution of their internal journey.

In "Hollywood-ending" movies, the external journey can end positively or negatively, but the internal journey always ends positively; this is what gives American films their heart.

Disney's *Tangled* follows classic *myth*ological structure, but places the *drama*tic emphasis on Rapunzel's individual need for freedom from her imprisoning mother (as opposed to focusing on the importance of becoming a woman who sacrifices her ego to make her present world a better place). In the end, Rapunzel *is* willing to give up her life for the one she loves, but the story ends with a eucatastrophic moment in which our heroine not only defeats the villain, but also gets everything she ever wanted and the story concludes with the narrator delivering the all-to-familiar *fairytale* line, "and they all lived happily ever after."

Americans place high value on happiness, a deeply *internal* human state. This is why nearly all American films integrate the internally driven genre of drama into their structures. Drama is a genre that places less emphasis on the external world of the main character, but relies heavily on the protagonist's internal journey. You will be hard-pressed to find a popular film that completely lacks an internal journey. Even in pure dramas, the main character usually still has some semblance of an external objective that they have to accomplish, but it takes a back seat to the internal objectives of the main character. *Tangled* is a story that has external journeys, internal self-actualization, and a happy ending. *Tangled* is a drama/myth/fairy tale. And this trifecta of story structure serves as the basis for nearly all Hollywood films and we call that, the American myth.

American myths are difficult to write in short form due to the combination of myth and drama – two genres that are strikingly different from each other. Lengthy amounts of time are required to effectively tell stories that follow the American myth model because they require a substantial amount of narrative information to communicate successfully. This is one reason why many short filmmakers exasperate themselves trying to emulate the films they see in American cinemas. There is just too much story information imbedded in an American myth to effectively communicate in an abbreviated amount of time. Short films work best when they stick to one genre; it keeps the structure and objectives of the story simple and streamlined. With that said, it is not impossible to tell an American mythic story in a short film, as we will see in the next chapter, but it is exceptionally difficult.

For better or worse, the American myth lost the original rhetoric of ancient myth. We rarely understand deep history by looking at the stories we once told, but rather we learn who we were by looking at the reasons *why* we initially told those stories. For millennia, humanity thought it was necessary to teach young men that they really weren't all that important, that they should give back to their community and that they should accept the fact that ultimately they were going to die and be forgotten. Can we glean wisdom through these old stories that seem so out of touch with modern, Western civilization? Regardless of whether or not we can, I think it important for all storytellers to ask themselves, not only why they like to tell stories, but why they feel compelled to tell the specific stories that they tell.

One of America's quintessential hybrid myths is the story of Dorothy Gale and her magical trip to the Land of Oz. The film, *The Wizard of Oz*, follows the structure of the novel with relative precision. L. Frank Baum made it very clear in his preface that he intended to tell a story that "aspires to being a modern fairy tale in which the wonderment and joys are retained and the heartaches and nightmares are left out." It is the "leaving out" of heartaches and nightmares (or the consequential "fourth act") that uniquely defines the American myth.

# CHAPTER SEVEN
# STORY BEATS FOR SHORT FILMS

*Finding the Foundation of Your Story and Your Main Character*

In this chapter, we are going to take a close look at Blake Snyder's 15 Beats from his book *Save the Cat*. In his story seminars, Snyder was notorious for showing students how his 15 Beats could be found in films of all lengths, from a two-hour movie all the way down to a thirty-second television commercial. Despite the power of this illustration, we have found that incorporating all of Snyder's beats into a short film can be difficult... and sometimes unnecessary. Snyder's 15 beats, John Truby's 22 steps, Chris Vogler's 12 stages of the hero's journey are all abridgments of Joseph Campbell's monomyth. These structures serve as road maps to help writers construct story-journeys for their heroes, journeys that mirror the psychological process of the human mind when it is confronted with and has to solve a problem.

To depict this honestly, a good writer should incorporate into their stories as many elements of the hero's journey as possible; however, it's important to realize that in any well-constructed story, hitting all of these elements might not be possible without your film feeling forced or inauthentic.

All well-constructed stories actually tell two stories – the INSIDE story of the hero, as well as their OUTSIDE story, which means all stories actually have two endings. As we discussed in the American myth chapter, most Hollywood stories are both mythic and dramatic in nature. The mythic story relies heavily on the outside story of the main character; whereas, the dramatic story relies heavily on the inside story. To incorporate both drama and myth into a short film is very difficult; more than likely, one of the stories is going to suffer and it's usually the inside story.

In a story-driven short film that relies heavily on mythic structure, your inside story is more than likely going to be light. Do not attempt to tackle deeply complex, emotional stories in short films, unless that's the only thing you're trying to do. Short films can be deeply moving and tackle the heaviest subject matters if your film is a pure drama, but as soon as you try to add a complex external (mythic) journey to drama, your short film suddenly becomes a feature. Although most story-driven films will have both inside and outside stories, just know that more than likely you will have to heavily favor one over the other.

So, let's take a look at Snyder's 15 beats – the structure that many Hollywood screenwriters use to build their screenplays. Snyder's 15 beats summarizes the structure of the American myth, a story structure difficult (but not impossible) to do in short films. So, after we break down Snyder's beats, we will whittle the 15 beats down to a more manageable eight – the eight crucial beats necessary for short films.

Snyder uses the term "beat" very liberally. In some cases, his use of the word refers to a VERY specific moment in the story, but some of his beats refer to entire sections of a film. For example, the *Fun and Games* beat is actually 25% of your film, whereas the *Break into Two* beat is usually a very specific moment. Don't get too hung up on this term.

Although it is possible to include all of Snyder's 15 beats in even the shortest films (in seminars, Snyder used to show a 30-second soap commercial, in which he pointed out all 15 beats), doing so effectively can be very difficult. We have identified the beats which are absolutely necessary for students to hit.

Act One is 25% of your film, Act Two is 50% and Act Three is 25%. This applies whether you're writing a two-hour feature or an eight-minute short. If they're going to do an eight-minute film, then their first act can only be two pages! And there's a LOT of storytelling that needs to happen in those two pages!

### 1. OPENING IMAGE:

The Opening Image is the first of Snyder's 15 beats. Not to spoil the ending, but the last beat we will discuss is the FINAL IMAGE. It's a good practice, especially in short films, to begin and end your movie with similar images. This way, your audience can easily contrast your main character's NEW normal with their OLD normal – how is life different now that our character has gone on this journey?

The opening image lets us know a few things about the film. It reveals the movie's genre, the story world, the world before our hero goes on their journey, and it sets the tone of the film.

It's also important to note that the Opening Image may refer literally to the first image we see, but more often than not, it refers to the opening scene.

### 2. THEME STATED:

This beat happens early in the story. The statement of the theme is usually a specific line of dialogue spoken directly TO the main character, not BY the main character. The theme usually has to do with the *internal problem* of the main character. It's a foreshadowing of the lesson the character is going to learn on his/her journey. If your main character already knows the theme of the film before their journey begins, then the journey is pointless and you have no story. A story is about a character discovering that theme for themselves.

### 3. SET UP:

This is one of those beats that encompasses a large portion of the film. *The Setup* is really your entire FIRST ACT; it includes *The Opening Image,* the *Theme Stated,* and all of the subsequent beats in Act One. *The Setup* is a very appropriate name for this section of the film, because that is exactly what you're doing; you are setting up questions (pertaining to the plot and the internal problem of the main character) that you're going to answer later on.

### 4. CATALYST:

This may be the single most important structural element in your entire story. Without this moment, you don't have a story. This is the moment that the *external goal* is first presented to the main character. It's an invitation to go on a journey. This beat may have been referenced in other books as "The Inciting Incident" or "The Call to Adventure." One important thing about this beat is the fact that, in a story world, the catalyst moment is never one that the main character can conjure up on their own; it has to be something presented to them by a secondary character. The main character doesn't find an adventure; it is presented to them.

### 5. DEBATE:

The Debate beat is the section of the film that occurs after the main character is invited to go on the journey, but before they actually decide to go. In the movie *Star Wars,* R2-D2 delivers Princess Leia's message to Obi-Wan Kenobi; Obi-Wan turns to Luke and says, "You must learn the ways of The Force if you're to come with me to Alderaan;" this is the catalyst moment in *Star Wars.* But, Luke turns to Obi-Wan and says, "I'm not going with you to Alderaan." He then proceeds to make up a few excuses why he can't go on the adventure and then turns to leave. And, for the next six-and-a-half minutes of the film, it seems like Luke is not going to embark on this amazing adventure.

But, after discovering that his family was killed by Imperial Storm troopers, Luke changes his tune. He returns to Obi-Wan and delivers one of the most important lines in the entire movie; without this line, there would be no *Star Wars*. And, that crucial line of dialogue **is** our next beat.

### 6. BREAK INTO TWO:

After experiencing the insufferable pain of the loss of his family, Luke nearly restates Obi-Wan's catalytic line of dialogue verbatim; he turns to Obi-Wan and says, "I want to come with you to Alderaan. There's nothing for me here now; I want to learn the ways of The Force and become a Jedi like my father." This is the moment Luke decides to go on the journey. We've just spent the first 25% of the film learning about Luke and the potential problems he might have to face, but it's not until he delivers this line that the story actually begins.

Classic Three-Act Structure refers to this moment in film as "Plot Point #1;" Joseph Campbell calls it "Crossing the Threshold;" and although John Truby's theories do not rely on traditional Three-Act Structure, he, too, has a special name for this moment in a story that he calls, "The First Revelation and Decision." We often refer to this moment as, "Crucial Decision #1." Story theorists have differing opinions when it comes to determining which moments in stories should be considered indispensable, but we all agree that without this particular moment, there would be no story.

### 7. B-STORY:

It's difficult to have a B-story in a short film, because there just isn't a lot of time. But, if you're going to have one, it begins during the beginning of the second act. A good B-story is not just a secondary story, but also one that parallels the A-story and supports it. It re-emphasizes the themes of the A-story and is often allegorical or metaphoric of the main journey upon which our hero is embarking.

### 8. FUN AND GAMES:

This is also a beat that time may not permit in a short film. Act One of the story is filled with tons of story information. By the time we get to the second act, your audience might be overwhelmed. The *Fun and Games* beat (which, like the setup, encompasses the entire first half of the second act) is the portion of the script in which the main character is progressing toward their goal, but we give our audience a break. We back off just a bit on the relentless storytelling. We give our audience a chance to breathe.

In the *Fun and Games* section of the film, the main character pursues their goal, but they pursue it at their leisure – the antagonist has not yet put on the pressure. Most of the tests our main character faces during this section of the film, our hero is able to pass. According to Snyder, this is also the section of the film that delivers on the promise of the movie poster (or the genre). If you are watching a sci-fi film, there is probably going to be a big space battle during this section of the film. In a slasher-film movie, the fun-and-games section might not be fun at all – lots of people probably get slaughtered during this section of the film. And in a musical, expect to see a big song-and-dance number once the second act begins.

### 9. MID POINT:

This is not one of the crucial short-film beats, but if you DO have a *Fun and Games* section in your short film, you should also have a mid point. This moment should literally happen in the middle of your film. In an eight-minute short, this moment should happen at the bottom of page 4/top of page 5.

This is a moment that changes the game; it refocuses the main character on their goal and suddenly, time becomes of the essence. The mid point usually comes about because of something proactively aggressive that occurs at the hands of the antagonist, or it can be a completely random event (CAUTION: use "random events" sparingly in your films).

Usually your main character has to make a decision at this point. Do they continue on or do they go home?

### 10. BAD GUY CLOSES IN:

This is the moment in the story when the bad guy begins his/her relentless attack on our main character. The pressure is on and things begin to fall apart. If we were watching the story from the antagonist's point of view, this would be the point when the antagonist begins to see the main character as an actual, legitimate threat and so, they start attacking with greater fury.

It's important to note that in the *Fun and Games* section of the film, the main character is basically passing every test they encounter, but usually they're passing these tests dishonestly. They win by cheating; they succeed because of beginner's luck; or they rely on emotional crutches for support. They are unaware of their dishonesty during the fun-and-games section. They begin to become overly confident, because things seem to be going their way.

But during the bad-guy-closes-in section of the film, all of that changes. Now our character begins to fail the tests that are put before them. The tests are more advanced and require greater knowledge. This is also the portion of the script when the main character is often abandoned by their friends.

### 11. ALL IS LOST:

This is also called the "False Defeat." The bad guy delivers a powerful blow that seems too great for our hero to bear. It appears to the audience that the victory has been lost and our main character has been defeated.

### 12. DARK NIGHT OF THE SOUL:

Just after the *All is Lost* beat, our main character wallows in their defeat. At this point, surrender seems to be the best answer for our hero. Even the hero suspects that it's for the best if they just go back home.

But our character doesn't remain in this state for long. Eventually, they pull themselves from the ashes and continue on. It is not uncommon for one of the main character's friends to encourage the hero not to give up. This secondary character usually "connects the dots" for the main character; they tell the hero that they've learned great lessons on their journey and that they have more strength than they realize. It's at this point the main character puts the pieces of the puzzle together and decides to finish the journey… even if it means they are going to die.

### 13. BREAK INTO THREE:

The break-into-two beat is the moment in the story when the main character proactively stands up and says, "Let's go on this journey!" This is why we refer to this beat as "Crucial Decision #1." Our character makes a conscious decision to start the adventure.

Likewise, the *Break into Three* beat is the moment when the main character stands up and makes "Crucial Decision #2" by saying, "Let's END this journey!" This is when the main character decides that defeat and giving up are not options. They are going to see this journey through to the bitter end.

### 14. FINALE:

In classic storytelling, this is when the main character faces their greatest moral test. This is the moment when the character must put into practice all the lessons they have learned. They no longer can cheat their way through, nor can they rely on beginner's luck or crutches. They have to stand up to the antagonist and face their internal weakness. Often the defeat of the antagonist is dependent on the main character overcoming their internal weakness.

In most stories, the hero wins, but it doesn't always have to go that way. Writing endings in which the protagonist loses are very difficult to write. Sometimes, beginning writers end their stories tragically just to avoid being cliché. This is horrible writing! A good tragic story should be masterfully constructed; it should play out honestly and, in the end, the "unhappy ending" should feel like the appropriate ending for the movie, not a gimmick.

### 15. FINAL IMAGE:

As we discussed at the beginning, the *Final Image* is the moment in the story that shows us our main character's NEW normal. Audiences would feel dissatisfied if we ended a story directly after the main character accomplished their external goal. Could you imagine if the credits rolled on *Star Wars* immediately after the Death Star exploded? How dissatisfying! Instead, Lucas treated us with an awards ceremony scene; we got to watch Luke revel in his victory alongside his friends.

According to film producer Lindsay Doran, one of the most important elements of a satisfying ending is that moment at the end of our hero's journey when we get to watch our main character share in their victory with the people around them. Have you ever been alone and experienced a beautiful sunset or tasted "the best cup of coffee ever?" Those meaningful moments that we experience in solitude can be beautiful, but I'm sure we all can recall a few times in our lives when an experience somehow seemed "less" simply because we had no one with which to share it. The shared experience of a victory is important for your story to resonant.

Snyder's 15 beats are an excellent model to follow and we have seen some successful short films that have utilized all 15 beats. But we've seen far more short films get bogged down in their efforts to take their main characters on the full hero's journey in under ten minutes.

To successfully tell a complete story (and show Hollywood that you can take a character on a journey from point A to point B) in a short film, it is best to simplify as much as possible. As we have previously discussed, a story is simply a "character trying to solve a problem." That's it! So, in your short film, find one simple problem and stay focused on that one problem.

In film, the external problem is always the character's need to accomplish their external goal. One of the main differences between shorts and features is the manner in which the external goal unfolds. In a feature film, it is possible for the external goal to start out very broadly and become more defined as the story progresses. For example, in the movie *Star Wars* at the end of Act One, Luke Skywalker says that he wants to go with Obi-Wan to Alderaan and learn the ways of The Force. As Luke embarks on this journey, many conflicts force him to adjust his direction.

At the beginning of the film, Luke's goal is to help Obi-Wan deliver R2-D2 to the rebel alliance, but by the end of the film, Luke's goal is to destroy the Death Star, the largest battle station in the galaxy. When Luke was just a farm boy back on Tatooine, he didn't even know what a Death Star was. So, in a feature film, the external goal can morph and become more focused as the story progresses, but in a short film, there isn't time for this sort of organic evolution of your main character's external goal.

In a short film, it's important to give your character one clear goal – a specific goal that is established at the beginning of the film and never changes. This will help keep your stories simple and will not require feature lengths to accomplish. Next, give your character a clearly defined flaw; it can be anything, but make sure it's not a flaw that requires a master's degree in psychology (or two hours of movie watching) to understand. The more you can relate this flaw to the external problem, the more streamlined your story will be.

To keep your story-driven short films simple and accomplishable, make sure you include at least the following eight beats from Snyder's 15 beats:

1. **Opening Image** – shows us the world before the character goes on their journey.
2. **Setup** – establishes the character's internal flaw and the main problem of the story.
3. **Catalyst** – presents a new (never before thought of) solution to the main problem of the story – a solution that only the hero can achieve. It will require proactive movement on the part of the main character.
4. **Break into Two** – If there is any "debate beat" in your short, it's brief, just a moment of hesitation. In a short, our main character decides rather quickly to pursue the solution to the main problem of the story.
5. **Bad Guy Closes In** – There may not be time for a *Fun and Games* section in a short film. Part of the reason for this beat in a feature is to give audiences a break after being assaulted with tons of narrative information during the first act. In a short, we don't necessarily have this problem and can move relatively quickly to the antagonist's relentless at-

tacks. To be efficient with your storytelling, make sure that your antagonist's attacks are designed specifically to not only keep the hero from achieving their goal, but also to attack our character's internal flaw.

6. **Break into Three** – Just like in a feature, eventually the main character must decide to end the journey.
7. **Finale** – The antagonist delivers their final attack and the main character must overcome their flaw in order to win.
8. **Closing Image** – shows us the story world after the character has gone on their journey.

Despite the fact that we have seen this abbreviated version of Snyder's beats work very successfully for our students as they've structured their short films, we still encourage them to incorporate as many of the 15 beats as possible into their stories.

As helpful as these structures can be, they also can be confusing and frustrating if you are new to the storytelling process. Often our students come to their pitch sessions earnestly attempting to adhere to the above steps, but their stories still seem very flat. Anytime we encounter this problem, the first thing we encourage students to do is to return to their main character. Have they taken the time to fully develop a compelling, cinematic character with a flaw that needs to be fixed? If they haven't, they will always struggle with finding their story. If you don't know what your main character's inside flaw is, you're going to have a tough time knowing on what type of outside journey they should go. If you find yourself stuck, review the Six Crucial Character Questions that we covered in chapter three. Make sure you've thoroughly answered those questions before you try to write any sort of story.

Another way to streamline your writing process is by looking at the story through the eyes of the main character. To ensure that the character you've developed is prepped and ready to go on their own unique story journey (tailor made just for them), make sure they can pass the following test. Answer all of these questions as thoroughly as possible! These questions work great for both short and feature films:

## Prepping Your Character for the Story Journey

### BACKSTORY:
*The OLD Normal - The world before the story begins.*

1. (EXTERNAL PROBLEM) Does your story world have a central PROBLEM?

2. (PROTAGONIST) Do you have a specific CHARACTER who lives in this story world?

3. (INTERNAL PROBLEM) Does your character have an internal WEAKNESS that disables them from doing anything about the problem?

### STORY:
*Your story begins when your main character comes to believe in a NEW, never-before-considered solution.*

4a. Is there a very specific EXTERNAL GOAL (solution) to solve the problem?

4b. (INCITING INCIDENT) What is the specific moment in time when this EXTERNAL GOAL is presented to your main character?

5.  (ANTAGONIST) Is there an opposing character that uses your main character's internal weakness against them?

6a. (MEASURES THE STRENGTH OF YOUR STORY): Does your character have a personal relationship to the problem of the story world?

6b. Does your character have a great deal to lose if the problem isn't solved

7a. (CHARACTER'S WORLDVIEW): What is your character's PERSPECTIVE of the story problem?

7b. How does your character typically SOLVE PROBLEMS?

## DENOUEMENT
*The NEW Normal - The world after the story ends.*

8.  BONUS QUESTION: Is the world (and your character) DIFFERENT after they've completed the story journey?

If you are still having trouble crafting your story, quit thinking about your plot altogether; focus your energy solely on developing your main character. Keep it simple; just answer the first four questions from the Six Crucial Character Questions. Create a very basic sketch. Many stories originate from a conflict between a character's ethics and their occupation. So, establishing your protagonist's career is a good starting point. If your character doesn't have a career, you should at least know what your character spends the majority of their time doing.

Once you have a rough sketch of your main character, begin experimenting with their outside goals, their inside goals, and the conflicts they will have to face as they pursue those goals. Play around; have fun! You will discover some interesting dynamics as you try new things. For example, come up with an inside goal for your main character like, "to find true love," but then experiment with different inside conflicts that prevent them from achieving that goal, like "fear" or "pride." You'll see that by changing the inside conflict, you will dramatically affect how your character perceives their inside goal. Try the same thing with the outside goal and the outside conflict (antagonist).

After you've found an iteration of goals and conflicts that you like, ask yourself this one, very crucial question, **"How far is my main character willing to go to achieve their outside goal?"** This is a very important and fun question to answer. Answering this question will more than likely determine the genre of your film.

For example, let's say your main character is a seventeen-year-old high school star quarterback whose external goal is to ask the most popular girl to prom. How far is this character willing to go to achieve his goal? Let's say he's willing to "wait patiently by the phone for the girl to call." What would the genre of this film be? What if he was willing to "slip a magical love potion into her coffee?" How does this change the genre? What if he was willing to "kidnap the girl's current boyfriend and hold him prisoner in the school basement?" As you can see, by addressing this very important question, not only can you come up with some interesting story ideas, but you also greatly affect the genre, the mood, and the tone of the film.

The process of writing is an organic one. There is no "one size fits all" approach that will always reap perfect results. You will discover that it is nearly impossible to develop the outside story of your main character completely independently from your character's inside story and vice versa. As you change one thing here, it affects another thing there. Paul Thomas Anderson once said that writing is like ironing a shirt. You move forward, but then you go back over the last little bit that you just ironed. Then you move forward a little further with the next pass of the iron... and back over the last little bit once again. The process continues - two steps forward, one step back, two steps forward, one step back. Slowly but surely, as you remain committed to the process; work though the psychology of your character; take them on a journey that challenges their internal weakness; poise them against an antagonist ready to attack; and craft cinematic moments that reveal your character's worldview. You will eventually make your way to the end and have a story that you can be proud of... and a story ready for the cameras to roll.

# CHAPTER EIGHT
# COMMON PROBLEMS – THE USUAL SUSPECTS

Before we address common problems in story-driven short films, it would behoove us to mention that most problems are a result of ignoring one of the structural rules or principles we have already covered. In our experience, most problems with short films occur because of a failure in one of the following basic principles:

- There is not a clear protagonist and/or antagonist
- The protagonist does not have an EXTERNAL goal
- The protagonist has an external goal, but it is not specific enough
- The stakes and/or conflict are not high enough to keep the audience interested
- There is no urgency to accomplish the protagonist's goal

We will look at each of these common story failures and explore ways to address them.

## THE STORY LACKS A CLEAR PROTAGONIST AND/OR ANTAGONIST

If you have determined that you are working in the realm of realism and that you are trying to create a character, concept or story-driven film, you need a clear protagonist. One of the most-oft uttered phrases when we critique short films is, "I wasn't sure whose story that was." Most times, when asked, the filmmaker is unsure of the answer to this as well. This can occur in a story for a vast number of reasons. However, one of the most common is that the filmmaker had a concept for their film and really didn't develop the story out of who the character was. Once, we even had a filmmaker admit to us that he really just wanted to make a zombie film and wasn't greatly concerned with the characters or story at all. While most filmmakers are not this candid and will try to defend their shortcomings with characters and story, the draw of creating a certain genre or concept in a film can be overwhelming, causing us to throw to the wind the elements of what makes a story effective.

This is not to say that a good story can't come out of a concept. Many of the greatest stories of all time started with a simple concept. However, those storytellers were faithful then to do the heavy lifting when it came to character development. Truthfully, it rarely matters if you begin with a character or a concept when it comes to storytelling. If you start with a character, eventually you will have to go through the process of developing plot. In the same way, if you begin with a concept, you then will need to go through the process of developing characters. Both are equally important.

Regardless of where you begin with your story construction, it is best if you eventually can land with a well-developed protagonist to be our focus as the journey unfolds. There are, of course, exceptions to this, such as stories that function with an ensemble cast, as well as romantic comedies where both characters may function as protagonists. We will deal with these exceptions later in the chapter. The majority of stories told through short film would benefit from focusing on a single protagonist and their journey, especially if that short film is being used as any sort of stepping stone into feature films.

While not as necessary as a protagonist, many short films do not have impact because they lack a human antagonist. While some shorts can succeed with simply an antagonistic force, it is often more powerful to have that force portrayed in human form. Even stories whose central conflict is man vs. nature (such as JAWS) will utilize a human antagonist (the sheriff) in order to increase conflict and make the story stronger.

We have seen a number of short films that feature antagonists that are not evenly well matched for the protagonists. The conflict in these films is always lacking. To review, here are a few characteristics of strong antagonists:

- **They are human**. This is assuming that the protagonist is human, of course. Whatever species or type of object the protagonist is, the antagonist needs likely to be the same. This assures the antagonist is well matched for the protagonist

- **They want the same thing as the protagonist**. This is why sports films work so well. The protagonist and antagonist want the exact same thing – to win the game. Having the same external goal forces the protagonist and antagonist into the same space, which raises the conflict. Remember, if your "bad guy" wants something different than your protagonist, they are likely a contagonist and not a classic antagonist.

- **They have a strong moral argument**. The best antagonists often have a very good reason for doing what they do. It is usually their methods that end up defining them. They often will demonstrate their failure to have truly learned the lesson in the theme of the film.

If you can work these characteristics into your antagonist, your story will always be stronger. If your story is not working, ask yourself the following question: "Do I have a clear protagonist?" "Will the audience have any trouble determining to whom I should be paying the most attention in this story?" "Can I clearly says this is a story about a guy or girl named _____ ?"

## THE PROTAGONIST LACKS AN EXTERNAL GOAL

Once you are sure your story has a protagonist, the next question you should be asking is, "Does this protagonist have an external goal?" For some reason, wrapping our minds around what is and is not an external goal can be extremely difficult for filmmakers. What we often think is an external goal is actually an internal goal. We have lost count of how many filmmakers we encountered that try to make the case that "finding love" is their protagonist's external goal. The fact that finding love is very much an internal journey (as external as that process might seem) eludes them. Here are a few tips to try and help you determine if you have an external goal or internal goal:

- **Can I take a picture of it?** Remember that we are working a visual medium. We have to be able to see the protagonist's goal accomplished. Merely seeing a protagonist smile or give "that look" is not an accomplishment of an external goal, unless, of course, that character's external goal WAS to smile or give "that look," which would likely make a very boring short film. If you are trying to justify a look or facial expression as the accomplishment of your protagonist's external goal, then you likely don't have an external goal.

- **Do the words LEARNS or REALIZES appear in my log line?** If either of these words is the active verb in your log line, you likely do not have a clear external goal. We cannot take a picture of someone learning or realizing something. We could. But we would have no idea this is actually what's happening inside their head. Learning something or realizing something is usually the result of the accomplishment of an internal goal.

- **Is the protagonist's goal something they must choose in order to accomplish?** Characters who are victims for the entire story or just have things happen to them make for very uninteresting characters. The circumstances these type of characters face affect their inner journeys more than their external journeys. We want to see characters make choices. The protagonist's external goal only should come about as a result of a decision they must make and the more difficult that decision is, the better. Great stories take us on the journey of a character who has to make a decision between two very desirable or undesirable choices. The more difficult this decision is, the higher the level of conflict in your story.

It is always a good idea to ask yourself what we are going to see this character actually DO in your story. If everything in your story revolves around conversations or your protagonist simply talking, you might not have a strong external goal. At the very least, your story might not be very visual. We watch films to see characters DO things. We want to SEE them accomplish goals and overcome odds.

## THE PROTAGONIST HAS AN EXTERNAL GOAL BUT IT IS NOT SPECIFIC ENOUGH

Perhaps you have determined that your protagonist has an external goal. Many filmmakers cease developing their external goal once they hit anything that is finite. For example, many writers have pitched to us that their external goal is for their protagonist to "get the girl." While a girl is certainly a photographable goal, we may ask ourselves, what

does it mean to "get" a girl? How do we know when the girl
has been "got"? Is it a first kiss? Is it that she claims to be the
protagonist's girlfriend or wife? "Getting" a girl is a very
vague external goal, partly because we cannot be sure exactly when and if this goal has been accomplished.

A more specific goal would be to secure a date with
a girl or to secure a first kiss. In most romantic comedies,
however, where we see a protagonist trying to "get a girl,"
there is usually another external goal that the character is
trying to accomplish while getting the girl. "Getting the girl"
is usually tied to the internal goal of the character, which is
"to find love" or something similar. Even if the character's
main end goal is to "get the girl," there is usually some sort
of metaphoric labyrinth that he or she must conquer to "get
the girl." This labyrinth is the external goal in these types of
stories.

Being ruthless with the question, "Is there any way to
make my external goal more specific?" always will lead to a
more defined path for the protagonist and a better story. The
fear most writers and filmmakers have when it comes to this
level of specificity is that the story will become boring or that
the stakes of the story will be lowered when the goal gets
this specific. If this is the result of making your external goal
this specific, you have just discovered a larger problem with
your story, which is a good thing. We shouldn't be afraid to
ask any question about our story that might reveal a weakness within it.

Another example of an external goal we hear often
that lacks specificity is when a protagonist's goal is to "get
away with" something. We have all seen stories about characters trying to get away with a big heist or fool everyone
else into thinking they are someone whom they are not.
These are wonderful stories often full of twists, turns and
intrigue.

However, rarely in these stories is the protagonist's goal to "get away" with whatever they are trying to pull off. Usually, whatever they are trying to pull off is a means to an end. That END is usually the external goal. We do ourselves a great favor to know enough about our protagonist to ask, "What is it they are trying to gain or secure if they get away with this?" No character is taking such great risks just for fun or just to see if they can. What is it they want that will cause them to go to such great risk? THIS will usually lead us to their true external goal. We should mention that in a feature film, there is more latitude in this arena. There is more time to develop a story about the journey. However, in a short film, the story is best served by a highly specific external goal beyond the character trying to "get away with something."

## THE STAKES AND/OR CONFLICT ARE NOT HIGH ENOUGH TO KEEP THE AUDIENCE INTERESTED

Perhaps the most common pitch we hear by filmmakers who believe they have an external goal for their short film is about the protagonist who must find their keys. A variation of this story is about a protagonist who must find a bathroom. Many filmmakers have pitched these stories because they are simple and do have a photographable external goal. We KNOW when the protagonist has found their keys. We can SEE when a character has found that elusive bathroom. However, because the take is so low in such stories, we are basically forced into repetition with our second acts. The character looks here for his/her keys, but they are not there. The character looks there for their keys but still can't find them.

Even when the character finds their keys, they will simply continue on with their life. There is nothing in the accomplishment of such an external goal that will bring about any true growth or change in our protagonist. The same holds true for the bathroom story. Even if our character finds a bathroom, they likely will need to find a bathroom again in a few hours. Nothing is really accomplished. We have simply hit the same beat over and over in our second act. The character might be temporarily relieved in the third act, but they have not grown in any significant way.

Here are some questions that we can ask to help us identify whether or not the stakes in our story are high enough.

- **Does my character's external goal have the potential to bring about growth in them or change them in some significant way?** If you are struggling to answer this question, it might be that the stakes in your story just aren't high enough. In order for an audience to want to go on a journey with us, they need to know it's worth their time. They want to believe that they will learn something about the way the world works or garner some nugget of truth, no matter how small. If the lesson that the character will learn on the journey (such as, be sure to use the bathroom before you leave the house) is one we already all know and lacks any debate or struggle; few will be interested in watching a character go on such a journey. Sure, the concept might be funny for about thirty seconds, but even the most talented filmmaker will struggle with making this interesting for two or three minutes, much less five or ten minutes.

- **What does my protagonist REALLY have to lose if they don't accomplish their goal?** If your protagonist's goal is just to find a date by Friday and they do not, what have they really lost? They likely will just keep looking the next week. However, if our protagonist must find a date by Friday to the Senior Prom, the stakes are much higher. The Senior Prom has potential to be something the character remembers the rest of their life. It only happens once. It has the potential to define how our character defines their high school experience for the rest of their life. The stakes are MUCH higher than simply finding a random date. If a character doesn't find their keys, they may be inconvenienced for the day, but life won't be greatly altered for them. However, if the key to their safety deposit box, which holds the deepest darkest secrets of their life has been stolen, suddenly the stakes are greatly raised.

- **Can we decrease the space and/or time in the story?** One of the oldest and most solid methods of raising the stakes in a story is to confine the space in which your protagonist has to accomplish their goal or decrease the time they have to accomplish it. We all have seen stories where the protagonist is just on the cusp of accomplishing their goal when suddenly, the antagonist locks them in a closet or basement. This method always will heighten the tension the audience feels for the characters to accomplish their goal. In the same fashion, "dropping a ticking time bomb" in the character's lap where the goal MUST be accomplished before the bomb explodes has always been an effective way to keep audiences on the edge of their seat and invested in the story.

## THERE IS NO URGENCY TO ACCOMPLISH THE PROTAGONIST'S GOAL

Suppose you have found the perfect external goal for your story. It is highly specific and the stakes are life and death. Now, suppose the protagonist has the rest of their life to try and accomplish the goal or solve their problem. Notice how this factor takes all the air out of our story's tires? If there is not some sense of urgency to our story, the audience will lose interest quickly.

This directly relates to what we just discussed about the "ticking time bomb." However, this concept goes beyond just raising the stakes of our story. Imagine if every second that our protagonist has not accomplished their goal leads to someone else's great suffering. This can lead to great development in our character. It can give them an underlying pain that drives everything they do. This begins to assist us in tying together a protagonist's external journey with their internal journey.

This example highlights the point that when the urgency of our story deals with a character besides our protagonist, it can cause more conflict for our protagonist. While it is certainly realistic to act in our own self-interest, it is usually more cinematic to act in the interest of others.

Here are some ideas to help you add urgency to the protagonist's goal:

- **Create urgency around the character for whom the protagonist cares most**. This has motivated heroes ever since there were heroes. How many of Superman's quests center on the fact that Lois Lane or Jimmy Olsen is in danger? It can be thrilling to watch a character save themselves. However, it is emotionally moving to watch a character risk and even sacrifice for someone for whom they care deeply. One rule of thumb for employing this technique is that the closer the character surrounded by urgency is to our protagonist, the more conflict. We intrinsically understand relationships with immediate family members and close friends. We do not have to use a great deal of story space to build the importance of such a relationship. This can help us create more efficient stories, which is especially helpful in short films. For this reason, urgency around the protagonist's brother will always trump urgency around their boss.

- **Wrap the urgency in a difficult choice for the protagonist.** It is said that compelling stories revolve around protagonists who must choose between two very attractive options or two very unattractive options. We see this trope play out all the time in cinema. Batman must choose between saving Rachel Dawes or Harvey Dent. He doesn't have time to save them both. He must choose. In the same way, romantic comedies often feature protagonists who must choose between the girl they want and the girl they need, usually very attractive options in more ways than one. If our protagonist is going to make a choice, it is far more interesting if that choice is going to cost them something. Not only is this compelling drama, it is often how real life works, which resonates with our audience. This technique is especially helpful in short film. An entire plot line can center around a difficult choice a protagonist must make. While this may not be enough conflict to hold a feature film together, it almost always is enough to hold together a short. One of the most powerful short films on which we ever gave notes centered around a young woman who was offered the college scholarship of her dreams in a faraway city. However, accepting it would mean leaving her ill mother with no one to care for her. Even in ten minutes, the agony of such a choice touches the heart.

- **Put the urgency in the hands of the antagonist.** Many of the examples we have mentioned thus far center around urgency that is handed to us by life. Another method of adding urgency is to have a character directly applying that urgency to our protagonist. The natural character for such a task is our antagonist. If our antagonist is the one setting the deadline for the protagonist's goal, it can bring about even greater conflict. All of us have a certain degree of sympathy and understanding for the urgency life occasionally hands us. It pushes an entirely different emotional button for a human being to intentionally be responsible for that conflict. While we all certainly have been guilty of causing urgency and conflict in the lives of others, we never seem to hold mercy for those who do such things in cinema. Utilizing this technique causes us to root even harder for the protagonist or form an even deeper hatred for the antagonist. Many films bring their audiences to an emotional climax by showing a protagonist overcome the urgent conflict set by the antagonist.

## OTHER FORMS AND EXCEPTIONS IN STORY

Finally, let's talk about something that many of you have wanted desperately to interject into this conversation – the exceptions. For every principle we outline in this book, there are exceptions. It is important to remember when dealing with story structure that we are talking about forms, not formulas. Even having an in-depth understanding of story structure does not necessarily make one highly skilled at executing these principles. Many of the greatest story gurus never have written a successful commercial script themselves. It is important to remember, however, that exceptions are just that – exceptions. MOST stories should fit within an established form. It has been our experience that many, if not most, storytellers who feel their work is the exception to established forms are actually inexperienced storytellers who have not put in the time or work yet to fully grasp how story forms work. It is surprising how many people we encounter who feel that their work is the exception to the rule and so

prolific that it transcends thousands of years of story principles.

It is a bit of a mystery why storytellers uniquely often
harbor these feelings. Musicians, and even architects, have
long accepted that there is an accepted form to their art. And
while one can push the boundaries of what might be popular at the time, you never see a musician trying to invent a
new chord that no one has used before. You just do not see
an architect trying to design a structure without any sup-
porting walls or columns. However, it is very common to see
storytellers trying to create stories without even a single established structural element. This being the case, let's discuss
some legitimate exceptions to the forms we have discussed.

## ENSEMBLE FILMS

Many filmmakers today tell stories because they were
greatly affected by the work of Robert Altman or Paul Thomas Anderson. Both storytellers have demonstrated great
skill in the art of creating ensemble films. Ensemble films do
not center around a central protagonist, but instead follow
the lives and journeys of a group of people. It is important
to note, however, that both of these filmmakers often have
taken over three hours to tell these ensemble stories. The ensemble film can be a highly effective form for telling a story
in a feature film. We have rarely, if ever, seen this form succeed in the short-film format. There just isn't enough time to
properly develop the characters and their journeys. It should
also be noted that even great ensemble filmmakers, such as
Altman and Anderson, showed great skill at telling stories of
single protagonists before they were given the opportunity
to tell ensemble stories. This type of filmmaking is for the
seasoned storyteller and not the short filmmaker still developing their own skills and style.

While we are on the subject of ensemble films, there is a hybrid form we have seen that can be effective, even in short film. Recently, we see this method utilized in comedy ensemble feature films, such as *The Hangover* and *Bridesmaids*. While both films are technically ensemble films, there are some common forms utilized by these films. First, films like these feature one character whose journey is really driving the story. The rest of the ensemble is providing support (and comic relief) for the journey. We have seen this method utilized effectively since early films like *The Wizard of Oz*. Next, while one character in the ensemble might grow, arc or learn a lesson, the other members of the ensemble are usually flat characters. Skilled storytellers have learned the value of having flat characters that serve a purpose in the story, but don't need to experience much of an arc in the story themselves. Finally, the four ensemble characters in *The Hangover* in some ways function as a single character with four sides (or personalities) going on a journey that follows very established story form and structure. This is actually just a variation on the established storytelling around which we have been building a case. As we have stated, these types of ensemble pieces can work in short film.

## STORIES WITH TWO PROTAGONISTS

Some stories seem to center around two protagonists who often have separate, but intertwining, journeys. One of the most common genres to feature such stories is the romantic comedy. We also see such scenarios in buddy-cop movies. Other story gurus have written extensively about these types of films. Blake Snyder's writing about the "Buddy Love" genre is especially exceptional. We also should mention that both these types of stories can work well within the short-film arena.

Let's look at the romantic comedy first. Even though at first glance, most romantic comedies seem to have two protagonists, most really have just one. There is usually one character whose goal is to establish relationship with the other character. One character is actively pursuing the other. In many cases, one character is acting as the protagonist and the other, as the antagonist. In the case of these stories, we simply have the traditional story form we have been discussing in this book.

We should mention that there is a difference between the romantic comedy genre and the romantic genre. Most times, in the romantic comedy genre, we do have a single protagonist who is driving the action. However, in the romantic genre, we may not. An example of a story from this genre would be *Romeo and Juliet*. The case easily can be made that both Romeo and Juliet act as protagonists in this story. However, they also act as a single unit throughout the story, even to their own demise. (Spoiler alert!) Romeo and Juliet really act as a single protagonist who battle against their parents, an ensemble who act as a single antagonist. This is the most common technique with the romantic film. Both protagonists will act as a single unit going on a single journey together. Their journey will usually follow the established story forms we have been discussing.

## ALL OTHER EXCEPTIONS AND FORMS

We can devote another book to exploring the exceptions to the "rules." While this might be a worthy effort, let us conclude this discussion with a few challenges to aspiring storytellers. First, learn to master the basics and established forms of storytelling before delving into the experimental and exceptional. Become a master of telling a simple, basic story before you charge into the dangerous waters of complex story structures and forms. If you come upon a partic-

ular story "rule" you don't like, see if you can master it. See
if you can become so skilled at executing it that you then
can demonstrate to others how and why it should be tran-
scended. Avoid the temptation to classify your work as the
exception. Instead, focus on becoming the most skilled in the
charted territories of story.

All of us get excited when we see a new storyteller
come along who brings something different to the discipline.
We all love to see people who advance the art form we love.
What we don't often see is the years of hard work that went
into learning the basics of the craft. We don't witness the
hours of study and practice spent by the filmmaker developing a style based out of the established work of others.
At some point in your storytelling, you will find the perfect
opportunity to break the "rules." Let that be the exception in
your work, not the established form.

# CHAPTER NINE
# THE END GAME

So, you've made your short film. You determined if you were making a realistic or abstract film. You discovered your film is story driven, as opposed to character driven or concept driven. You've even worked through the story forms of fairy tales, fables, myths and American myths and know where your film fits. You took time to develop the story. You have a protagonist with a clear, visual, external goal. You have an antagonist who wants the same thing, but has different methodologies of achieving it. You have all ten crucial story beats. What now?

So many filmmakers create shorts with either no end game in mind or such a lofty end game that no short could ever meet their expectations. We have lost count of the number of filmmakers we've encountered who plan to create the best short the world has ever seen, enter it in festivals, and then spend the next two years entertaining offers to direct a feature film. The truth is that there was an era when the possibilities of that happening were much greater. However, for the most part, that era is long over. Does this mean there isn't a way to parlay short films into a career in features? This certainly is not the case either. Just like every protagonist should have a goal in your stories, so should you when creating short films.

## DETERMINING A PURPOSE

With rare exceptions, the first short film that ANY-
ONE makes is not ready for the festival circuit. Oftentimes,
neither is the second or third effort. So if we aren't creating
shorts to win (or even be accepted into) festivals, why both-
er? Here are a few reasons to make a short film, even if the
end purpose is not to enter the film into festivals.

## PRACTICE. PRACTICE. PRACTICE.

One of the best reasons to be making short films is
for the practice. There is an often-told story in the industry
about a college-level pottery class. In the class, the professor
divided the students into two groups on the first day. He
gave the two groups different assignments for the semester.
The first group, he instructed to spend the entire semester
trying to create the perfect pot. He asked them to research,
analyze, and plan. He asked them to put a great deal of
thought into creating something that could be held up without flaws. The second group, he instructed to create as many
pots as possible over the course of the semester. He told
them not to overly concern themselves with the quality of
each pot, but only to focus on churning out as many as was
humanly possible. The two groups spent the entire semester doing as instructed. On the final day of the semester, the
professor asked the two groups to present their work. The
first group explained all their research and calculations in
trying to create the perfect pot. While the pot was good, the
class easily determined several flaws in the pot, despite the
group's best efforts to make it perfect. The second group
presented their work. They had created literally hundreds of
pots over the course of the semester. While most of the pots
had very obvious flaws, there were over a dozen pots that
the class determined were nearly flawless and had far fewer

flaws than the pot the first group had spent months trying to perfect.

For some reason, the idea of practice is not a popular concept in the story and film worlds. Other art forms have long recognized the importance of such disciplines. Most musicians spent hours and hours in practice before they ever attempt to take a musical composition to an audience. Most painters will never show patrons the hundreds of sketches and tests on which they toil away. However, many story-tellers feel perfectly comfortable sending out the first draft of a story or entering their first cut of a short film into every festival they can afford.

There is not enough that can be said on the value of practice. Nothing helps a storyteller more in figuring out for themselves what works and what doesn't. The more a storyteller practices, the finer their craft becomes. One of the best purposes a storyteller has for creating a short film is to practice. Even if a piece of work does turn out well and you decide to enter it into festivals, you are far better off begin-ning that venture with the purpose of practice in mind.

## DEMONSTRATING MASTERY OF A PARTICULAR SKILL

For many years, the only purpose in creating a short film at all was to create a calling card that would demon-strate a filmmaker's capability. In some ways, this is still true. However, short films have developed into their own art form, and now it might be argued that there are as many festivals and competitions for short films as there are for fea-tures. Storytellers have become wise in that short films can be used to demonstrate developed skills in a particular area. Here are a few skills that filmmakers might create a short film to demonstrate.

## THE ABILITY TO TELL A COHERENT STORY

If you have ever attended a short-film festival, you might have been surprised at how many films fell into the abstract, character-driven and concept-driven categories. Certainly there is nothing wrong with these types of films. What is interesting, as we have stated, is that most of these filmmakers are trying to use their projects to parlay into a career in feature films. However, what they fail to realize is that they have failed to show that they have the ability to tell a coherent story. Story-driven films with good structure at festivals are true rarities. This is not because they have been kept out of the festival. It is mostly because they are hard to find. Recently, we had a short film play at a block in a major festival alongside films with exponentially larger budgets and better-known casts. When we asked the festival programmers how we got so lucky, they told us that we actually had a story with a beginning, middle and end, which they don't see very often. Structure is what helped us get accepted into this major festival. If you want to use short films to eventually climb into the world of features, it is imperative that you demonstrate the ability to tell a good story.

## THE ABILITY TO CREATE A WORLD

Suppose the end game for your career is to write and direct feature-length science-fiction films. You likely will never get that opportunity without demonstrating, at some point, that you understand the creation of other worlds and have the skills to create a world of your own. Many filmmakers just assume when they have millions of dollars with which to work, they will suddenly develop the necessary skills to create the things they see in their head. While money certainly gives us more room to play, most filmmakers never gain access to such budgets because they have not demonstrated the ability to take the vision in their head to the screen on a smaller budget. Creating a world goes far beyond the ability to hire a talented production designer. If the world isn't first on the page, the production designer has nothing to execute. If, by some chance, the film does showcase a new world we haven't seen before, despite not being found in the story, it is a testimony to the production designer's skill more so than the storyteller.

## THE ABILITY TO CREATE INTERESTING CHARACTERS

This is where some filmmakers might choose to focus on creating a character-driven film as opposed to a story-driven film. Ideally, you could create a story-driven film that featured well-developed, interesting characters. However, as Billy Bob Thornton demonstrated in his early short film, *Some Folks Call It A Sling Blade*, filmmakers have been able to parlay feature films out of interesting characters, of whose story we only see a portion, within a short film. It should be noted that a film designed for that purpose should not only feature an interesting character, but also a character capable of development. It is important that we can imagine the character being able to carry a larger story than what we see in the short film. We need to be able to imagine the character having the ability to grow and the capability to change.

## THE ELUSIVE FESTIVAL CHAMPION

Finally, we must deal with the short film that has been created for the festival circuit. Even if a film is created with this purpose, the first question that must be asked is if the film is festival ready. It is extremely wise, before spending money to enter your film in a festival, to do a bit of research. Go back and track down the films that won previously at

that festival. This will give you an idea of what these particular festival programmers are looking for. If you feel your
film would fit well within this "family" of films, you must
ask yourself a brutally honest question. Is the quality of my
film up to par with the other films that won in the past. The
quality of short films seems to be rising every year. If your
film cannot match the quality of previous winners, it is unlikely the programmers will look to you to be the future face
of the festival.

It is quite difficult to be objective about our own
work. If you struggle with this, and most of us do, it is important to invite notes from those who you know will give
you honest critique. Far too many filmmakers spend twice
the amount they spent on their films to enter them into festivals in which they have no real shot of gaining acceptance.
Many films have glaring problems that keep them from
serious consideration by a festival because many filmmakers
are blind to the problems in their work. Here are some ideas
to help you get an honest evaluation of your story or film
before dropping lots of money on festival entries.

## FIND THREE HONEST CRITICS

You might be surprised at the number of filmmakers
who invite notes from people they subconsciously know
will heap praise on the film. All of us like to hear nice things
about our work. However, very little improvement or
growth comes out of this. Storytellers should seek out notes
from people who have a better-than-average understanding
of story. If that person actually has some training or experience in story and its structure, all the better. We have chuck-
led at the number of filmmakers who actually said to us
that their parents really like their story and believe it could
be successful. Relatives, close friends, and spouses mostly
should be excluded from your list of those you invite to give

you notes. We suggest at least three critics to give notes on your project. Why? Because this can be a very subjective process. Even the most seasoned story expert will offer their subjective opinions mixed in with established principles of story structure. If you receive a note about your story from one person, it is worth considering, but is not completely imperative that you take the note. If you hear the same note from two or three people, you can bet the majority of your larger audience is going to feel the same way about the story beat. You would do yourself a great favor to address the note.

## DETERMINE NOT TO GIVE DISCLAIMERS OR NEGOTIATE THE FEEDBACK YOU ARE GIVEN

There is something within us that feels the need to defend our work the first time people see it, especially if the work is still in progress. We have sat in literally hundreds, if not thousands, of notes sessions where the storyteller begins the session with a series of disclaimers. The problem with this is that filmmakers will not be present to give those disclaimers before a more general audience experiences the story. Even if they were, who would want to listen to a storyteller give reasons why their work may not be up to par before we even see the work. This might be the most difficult challenge we could issue, but determine not to give any disclaimers or negotiate with the note giver about your work. Actually, it is usually helpful to try and say as little as possible. Promise yourself only to listen and nod. This does not mean you have to take every note that is given. However, disciplining yourself not to argue your method or motivation creates an environment where the note giver will actually give you better notes, because they will be more honest. When the note giver senses pushback on each note they give, they begin to sensor and edit themselves internally, trying to create the least amount of conflict possible with you. Rarely do the best notes come out of such a session.

## BE WILLING TO DO THE HARD WORK OF FIXING PROBLEMS

This becomes especially important when you have heard the same note more than once. Unfortunately, most people ask for notes and really just want to be told how great the work is. Few people are actually up for trying to fix problems in the work. Commit yourself to addressing any note that you hear more than once. Addressing the note does not necessarily mean using the solution the note giver has offered. However, if they are a seasoned story person, their suggestion should be seriously considered. This is especially true if several of their notes are dependent on one another. Many times we have given notes on a story that all depended on our first suggested approach being followed. What often happens is that the storyteller will pick and choose a few of the notes we gave. However, because they didn't take our initial, suggested approach, the structure problems in the story remained. Rewriting can be harder work than writing itself. You must be willing to put in the time to continue the task, if you want the best story possible.

## FINAL THOUGHTS

Before we conclude, let us say a few final words about the end game of making short films. The approach in this book is to provide a path for those who want to use short film as means toward a career in film or at least a higher level of storytelling. However, it would be dishonest of us to suggest that the most important reason for becoming an excellent storyteller is so you can use that skill to make money. While this is the motivation of many, and it can be a wonderful benefit of developing this skill, creating any piece of art should be about the journey and the soul.

Strangely enough, even though the pursuit of money is what motivates a great deal of people in the world, that goal actually makes for a poor external goal in story. We will buy into the story of a protagonist whose goal is to get money, but only if that money is for some noble or necessary cause. When it is not, we almost always see that character as greedy and have difficulty identifying with them.

There is something mysterious and captivating about story. The more we learn about it, the more we realize what we don't know. Telling a compelling story actually feels like it transcends our humanity. It causes us to feel as though we are part of something greater. In so many ways, the pursuit of great story is its own reward. From a different angle, what good is a story without an audience to which to tell it? Seeing your story's impact on the faces of those to whom you are telling it brings a reward that money just cannot buy.

Tell stories. Tell lots of them. Don't tell them for money or for fame. Don't tell them for yourself or for personal benefit. Tell them for the benefit they might offer to others. Tell stories because you have something to say. Tell them because you have something true you want to share with the world. Tell stories. It's the most human thing you can do.

CPSIA information can be obtained
at www.ICGtesting.com
Printed in the USA
LVHW031154110119
603565LV00001B/294

9 780988 930568